Lunchbox Made Easy

RECIPES TO RAISE HEALTHY LUNCHBOX HEROES

BY SIOBHAN BERRY

Lunchbox Made Easy

RECIPES TO RAISE HEALTHY LUNCHBOX HEROES

BY SIOBHAN BERRY

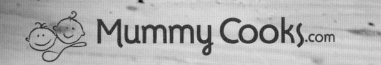

To my very own lunchbox heroes
Ashleigh and Jessica, my life,
my inspiration. Thank you for
being such a big part of my
Mummy Cooks journey.

© Mummy Cooks by Siobhan Berry, 2020
ISBN: 978-1-78972-000-6

Portrait Photography by Dave Berry
Food Photography by Shika Finnemore
Designed by Shika Finnemore
Edited by Laura Erskine & Fionnuala McLoughlin

Printed in Italy by L.E.G.O. SpA

A CIP Catalogue record of this book is available from the British Library.

www.MummyCooks.com

All content in this book is not intended to be a substitute for professional medical advice.
Always seek the advice of a qualified health provider with any concerns you may have about feeding your child.

Acknowledgements

Little did I know that a year after launching my first recipe book 'Baby & Family; Cook for Family, Adapt for Baby' I would be writing my second book. Many of my amazing loyal followers, whose babies I helped wean, now have school going children and face a whole new challenge of packing school lunches their children will eat. Thank you for inspiring me to write this book, I love that we can continue this journey and feed our children a healthy lunch.

To my beautiful and very patient daughters Ashleigh and Jessica. You both have been a very big part of writing this book. I adore that you love helping out in the kitchen and inspire me to come up with new and exciting recipes. Thank you especially for helping out with photoshoots, although not always fun you were happy to be part of the team.

The hardest part of writing this book has been finding the time to do it. For this I want to thank Dave, my very supportive husband, who has taken some amazing family photographs to add to my book. Thank you for being a great Dad to our two girls.

To Shika my designer, photographer, illustrator, editor…the list goes on. You should be very proud of this book, it is as much yours as it is mine. You understand us so well and make it so easy to work remotely as far away as Australia. Although you are now the other side of the world, I don't believe it is the end of your Mummy Cooks journey.

To my Mummy Cooks team past and present who have had a role in making this book. Thank you for helping me grow my dream and inspiring thousands of parents.

To all the experts that have helped me in writing this book. With special thanks to my sister Catriona, Paediatric Occupational Therapist. Thank you again for your guidance especially in writing about 'Engaging the Senses.' To my friend Laura Erskine, thank you for your editing skills. I really appreciate your guidance on this book and the last. I would also like to thank Aveen Bannon, Consultant Dietitian, for your support in writing this book and your glowing review of my recipes.

To Kevin and his team at Arena Kitchens, thank you for allowing us to carry out photoshoots in your beautiful kitchens.

Lunchbox Heroes

Through writing this book I wanted to not only inspire parents with my recipes but also empower children to get involved in creating their own lunchbox. These parents and children are our Mummy Cooks Lunchbox Heroes and we asked them to get involved and show us their healthy lunch creations. We were overwhelmed by the response and here is a selection of Lunchbox Heroes. Why don't you share your little one's creation by using #lunchboxheroes on social media.

"How to make a lunchbox tasty and healthy can be a challenge for many parents...but I am loving the suggestions and ideas that Siobhan offers here. There are a multitude of great nutritious colourful recipes along with some helpful tips on how to pack lunches and get kids involved with food. What I really love is that these are dishes that the whole family can enjoy. Overall a great cookbook with original and clever ideas that will create a fun and stylish lunchbox!"

**Aveen Bannon,
Consultant Dietitian**
@aveenbannon

"Siobhan's first book has been like a baby food bible for me, I especially love that it has recipes & ingredients that can be eaten by the whole family and sourced in local Irish supermarkets. There are lots of inspirational recipes with food combos that I wouldn't think of myself. My little lady absolutely loves her food and I can hands down say a lot of it was the variety I gave her thanks to Mummy Cooks recipe book. It's super handy for busy mamas."

**Charlene Flanagan,
Mum to Anna Gabrielle and Charlie**
@charleneflanaganmakeup

"I'm a reluctant 'cook' and really only started making meals from scratch when I felt I had to get good food into small kids. The first Mummy Cooks book changed my perspective, and I actually enjoy the challenge of mastering a new recipe now. All four of us inhale the dinners, and there's always a portion left over if I'm on a late shift in work which helps me make better food choices. Our favourites are the coconut chicken curry or the chicken twist on the traditional chili con carne! We can't wait to start using this book, just in time for having two kids at 'big' school."

**Evanne Ní Chuilinn
RTE Sport Broadcaster,
Mum to Séimí agus Peigí**
@evannenichuilinn

Contents

Introduction **12**

Advice **14**

Breakfast on the Go **47**

Soups **65**

Bread & Muffins **83**

Salads **105**

Sandwiches & Wraps **117**

Pasta & Sauces **135**

Pesto & Spreads **157**

Pancakes & Waffles **175**

Snacks **185**

Smoothies **203**

Treats **215**

Index **232**

Introduction

When my first daughter Ashleigh was a toddler, I thought it would be easy packing a healthy lunch every day. She was a great eater and finished meals with no fuss. However, once she started school a large portion of her food started coming home uneaten. She said she didn't have enough time during her short lunch break. Packing a lunch that would be eaten was harder than I anticipated!

As I spoke to other parents, I realised school lunches are the meal that many of us find most stressful. The more I discussed this issue, the more I understood the anxieties parents feel. We simply don't have enough time to be making healthy meals from scratch every morning. There is always such a rush to get the children ready and out the door, that taking the time to do so is just too unrealistic.

As a result, many of us feel helpless and are forced to resort to less healthy choices. If a child has developed picky eating habits this can especially push parents towards these less healthy choices just so their child eats something at school. I understand that it is so disheartening to feel stuck in this situation and I want to help.

This book is packed full of inspiration for nutritious, child-friendly lunches. From snacks to sauces to soups, I have included over 100 of my favourite lunchbox recipes. I want to offer a permanent solution to the lunchbox rut - one that will suit all parents! I have carefully considered how to pack a really healthy lunchbox that will suit every child, from the picky to the most adventurous. I want to give every parent the basic tools they need to change their school lunch routine for the better and empower every child to get involved in creating their own lunchbox and become a lunchbox hero!

Lunches don't have to be more stressful than any other meal to prepare. My philosophy for school lunches is the same that I apply for every single meal: preparation is the key to healthy, homemade food. As a working mum myself, I don't have time to be making meals from scratch in the mornings. If you read my first recipe book 'Baby & Family: Cook for Family, Adapt for Baby', you will know how passionate I am about batch cooking! Setting time aside once a week to cook a big portion of food for your family is the best form of meal prep. I guarantee it will save you time, effort and stress in the weeks to come. A little bit of organisation really does go a long way.

I hope my book inspires you to implement my advice into your school lunch routine. Small changes here and there can really make the world of difference. We all know that being a parent is easily the busiest job in the world, so I want to take the stress out of your weekly lunchbox plan. My aim is to soothe your anxieties, and let you know that you can pack a healthy lunch every day that your children will love. With just a little bit of organisation and planning, you'll soon find that this is an easy part of your daily routine.

Preparing for a Week of Healthy Lunches

The school morning is always a bit hectic! Amidst all of the rushing around, it's impossible to prepare a healthy lunchbox every morning from scratch. It is simply too time-consuming and unrealistic.

Food Preparation

As with almost all healthy eating, the key lies in preparing food in advance. So, my best advice is to batch cook. This means once a week (or even once a month, whatever suits you best), get in the kitchen and prepare food for the weeks ahead. Think of it as a little bit of time set aside to save you a lot of time in the future.

So what are the best foods to batch cook? I suggest stocking up on healthy homemade sauces. They are so versatile and can be enjoyed as dips, as spreads, stirred through pasta; the list is endless.

Basil & Courgette Pesto (page 158)

I always make sure I have a big batch of my Marinara sauce in the freezer. The night before I need some, I place it in the fridge to defrost. Then in the morning all I have to do is prepare some pasta, heat the sauce and mix it in; creating a delicious lunch in only ten minutes. On other days I use Marinara sauce as a dip for savoury muffins or chopped vegetables. Having a reliable recipe that is versatile makes planning school lunches much easier. Ask your child what their favourite sauces are so you can batch cook them.

Sauces you can batch cook:
Marinara Sauce pg 148
Quick Bolognese pg 137
Tomato & Mascarpone Sauce pg 150
Spicy Tomato Sauce pg 155
Pestos pg 157
Hummus pg 166-167

Stock up on essentials

A really easy way to be prepared in advance is to have your go-to ingredients on hand at all times. This advice may seem obvious, but I cannot emphasise enough how much easier planning a lunch is when you are consistently on top of the shopping list. Plan a food shopping trip at least once every week, and make sure you are aware of what weekly essentials you need.

It is important that when you are shopping you understand the need for variety. This means that when buying pantry staples, you are buying them in a few different forms. It's even important to mix things up like the variety of breads (page 83) you use, as children can quickly get bored of eating the same foods every day. Make sure you have a wide range of proteins, from cheese and yoghurt to turkey and ham. All in all, you want a large enough amount of choice in each food group so that you can guarantee that your child's lunchbox varies every day of the week. Even if your child has a favourite food you should avoid packing it more than every two days or your child may eventually reject the food.

Preparing snacks

Snacks are also important to your lunchbox plan (recipes from page 185). Homemade snacks are really easy to batch cook. Simply double the ingredients of whatever recipe you are using and you will have enough for weeks to come.

Muffins, for example, are an ideal snack to prepare in advance. They freeze exceptionally well, and are easy to bake in bulk. All you have to do is defrost them in the fridge overnight or in the microwave in the morning before school. Muffins are wonderful to pack full of nutritious fruit and vegetables, making them great when encouraging picky eaters to get in their five a day. In our house, one of the few foods my girls don't like are bananas. They do however really enjoy my Apple and Banana Muffins (page 92), so I make them to get potassium into their diets!

Of course, at times you may find it easier to buy snacks and that is perfectly fine. Just make sure that what you are buying is low in salt and sugar content. Check out page 38 on reading food labels.

A few snacks you can batch cook and freeze:
Muffins pgs 89-93
Cheese Scones pg 85
Fruit Breads pgs 101-103

Leftovers

Don't forget that leftovers are perfect for lunch too. Children often prefer a cooked lunch like pasta over a sandwich, so using leftovers is a really easy option. Making Cauliflower Macaroni and Cheese (page 147) for dinner? Just make a little extra and fill up a food flask with some the next morning. Planning school lunches does not need to be complicated at all, it just requires forethought.

Lunchbox Checklist

Everything you need to make packing school lunches as easy as possible!

Lunch & Portion Pots

Always place different foods in separate pots. This is particularly important for fussy or picky eaters. Having enough pots lets you have things like your snacks and fruit portioned out and ready for the week. Things like muffins, dips and sauces can be batch cooked and frozen in advance in the right size pots to make your mornings easier.

Here are four lunch pots that are perfect for preparing your child's lunchbox. My Mummy Cooks Lunch Set includes five of each size, so you have enough pots to prepare for the week:

16oz/480ml - sandwiches, pitas, wraps

6oz/180ml - yoghurts, vegetable sticks, fruit

8oz/240ml - muffins, snacks, fruit

3oz/90ml - dips, sauces, seeds

Lunch Bag

Make sure your lunch bag has plenty of room for pots and a food flask. Try not to get anything that is too rigid and make sure it can be easily washed which saves time! There are so many adorable designs available, so let your child show their personality off. Once they choose their own, they will be excited to bring their lunch to school every day.

Food Flask

My Mummy Cooks food flask is essential to my lunch plan. The ability to pack hot lunches or keep food cold allows for much more versatility and creativity. With this, I can pack pastas, soups, smoothies and so many other tasty meals that I otherwise couldn't. My 300ml flask is the perfect portion size for a school going child. Make sure you fill your food flask to the top to ensure the food stays warm.

A Fork & Spoon

You'll need cutlery, especially when using a food flask. Buy a child-friendly set that is reusable if you are reluctant to send them off with your best cutlery. It will also make them feel like a real grown up!

A Water Bottle

It is important that your child gets a bottle of water in their lunch bag every day. Hydration is vital, especially for young children so make sure they are drinking it all. Buy a reusable bottle that you can wash instead of sending in disposable ones every day, as this reduces waste. When buying, make sure that the bottle is a fairly simple design without too many plastic add-ons such as straws. These can make them much harder to clean and encourage bacteria to grow. Also, make sure that your child can manage to open and close it without difficulty. Younger children in particular can struggle, so providing a bottle that is easy for them to use will prevent leaks.

Building the Perfect Lunchbox

The key to the perfect lunchbox is balance. This means that every day, your child is getting at least one item from the three main food groups in their lunchbox: carbohydrates, protein, fruit and/or vegetables. Including all food groups also ensures your child gets their fibre intake. Eating foods rich in fibre helps prevent constipation and safeguards against other bowel problems.

Carbohydrates

Carbohydrates are used in the body to make glucose, which is our main energy source. In my experience, this is the easiest group to encourage your child to eat. Few children object to bread or pasta however, they may not like wholemeal versions - particularly in pasta form. If you want to introduce more wholemeal options into your child's diet, a good compromise is the half and half method. Simply use both white pasta and brown pasta when cooking their lunch, and swirl in a tasty sauce. The mix of the two will seem a lot less scary to your child and will gently ease them into eating wholemeal.

Most children are very responsive to bread, so I would take advantage of this to experiment with a variety of types. Head to the bread aisle and take some time exploring the many choices available or better still bake your own breads (page 83), this is easier than you might think! Pitas, wraps, toasted sandwiches - there are so many ways to keep this category exciting and new. Sandwiches are also the perfect vehicle for introducing wholemeal so look out for different types of seeded and wholemeal bread.

Protein

Protein is essential for healthy muscle, bones, skin and building tissue in our bodies. This is why it is really important that your growing child gets a portion in their lunchbox every single day. When most people think of protein, they automatically think of meat. However, did you know just how many other foods are also great sources? Cheese, eggs, yoghurt and beans are all packed with protein, and having a wide range of options on hand is a helpful way of increasing variety in this category.

Proteins are often really easy to prepare. Keep some hard-boiled eggs on hand in the fridge, and pop one into your child's lunchbox during busier days. Omelette fingers are great too, and are a quick option to make from scratch. Nuts are also packed with protein and many children adore nut butters, so I've included a recipe for nut butter on page 173 - it's so easy to make! While it's perfectly fine to spread these on bread, it's also nice to have a little fun with some child-friendly recipes. My Peanut Butter Cookies on page 217 have only three ingredients, and no child will object to a biscuit for their snack! Just remember to take note of any policies on nuts in your child's school as some children are severely allergic.

18

Fruit and/or Vegetables

In my experience, speaking to many parents, fruit and vegetables cause the most difficulty when packing a child's lunch. Please don't panic if you're struggling! There are many ways to help your child embrace this food group.

You can make a world of difference by simply changing up how you serve fruit and vegetables! Serve vegetable sticks with your child's favourite dip - this is much more appealing than just chopped vegetables on their own. Cutting colourful produce into circles and squares also looks visually fantastic in a lunchbox. Never underestimate just how much children judge food by how it looks. If this is a tricky food group for your family, then you have to remember to keep things fun.

Don't forget, your fruit or vegetable portion does not always have to be served in its original form. Sauces can be packed with a variety of nutritious produce. This makes them especially great if your child is initially extremely unreceptive towards vegetables. Simple recipes such as my Marinara Sauce contain a multitude of amazing superfoods, such as tomatoes, peppers, cauliflower and butternut squash, blended to a sneakily smooth consistency (page 148). Similarly, pesto is always a hit with children and can be made with healthy greens such as courgette (page 158).

Avoid packing the same options every day. This can get very boring for your child and can cause them to food jag (page 36). Have six or seven forms of produce in rotation to keep lunchtimes interesting. This doesn't even have to be a very wide variety if your little one is fussy. Remember fruit like oranges and apples come in many forms. A big, juicy orange cut into segments is very different to a compact mandarin orange. Apples also come in such a vast range, from a bright green Granny Smith to a Pink Lady, they all taste quite different. You can even serve a variety of flavours in one go by fashioning a fun fruit kebab or packing a fruit salad. Little details like this make the lunchbox colourful and enticing.

Another key factor when packing fruit and vegetables is to make sure that your child can easily manage them. This may sound obvious but it is something often overlooked! If an apple comes home with only a few bites taken from it, it may be that it was simply too big for your little one to handle. Learn from this and next time cut the fruit up or offer a smaller size. With grapes and cherries, always make sure they are seedless or pitted. Perhaps peel the more difficult fruit and vegetables if your child prefers them that way. You don't want anything to stop them from enjoying fruit and vegetables, so make the experience as easy as possible for them.

Spinach

tomatoes

beetroot

cucumber

courgette

peppers

sugar snap peas

broccoli

cauliflower

Try to include at least one vegetable

Crunchy - sticks of veg
Smooth - spreads
Chunky - soups

carrots

green beans

aubergine

mango

strawberries

apples

pears

oranges

blueberries

raspberries

lime

blackberries

peach

lemon

Try to include at least one fruit as a snack

Sweet - pears, pineapple, apples, berries
Bitter - grapefruits, oranges, lemons, limes
Blended - fruit smoothie

banana

pineapple

ham

chicken

chorizo

Protein

tuna

lentils

nut butter

nuts

seeds

Try to include at least one protein

Crunchy - nuts, seeds, chickpeas
Creamy - soft cheese
Meaty - chicken (tender), chorizo (chunky)

dairy

cheese

Including Your Child in Making Their Lunch

The best way to encourage your child to eat a healthy lunch is to get them involved in making it. While doing so, it's important to help them understand what is involved in making it healthy as well as delicious. You can use my photo guides from pages 20 to help you explain what belongs in each food group and how meals need to be balanced.

When making their lunch, let your child pick an item from each category: at least one carbohydrate, one protein, one fruit and/or vegetable. I talk a lot in this book about pairing 'comfortable' preferred foods with 'uncomfortable' less favoured foods. This is one of the best methods for helping your child overcome fussy eating habits. A lunch solely made up of foods that your child is uncomfortable with will only discourage them and may even put them off the whole meal. If there are some foods that they are happily familiar with, it will ease them in gently and they are more likely to try new things. By laying out their lunch options into categories, you encourage them to pair the comfortable with the uncomfortable. For example, if they are not fans of protein but love carbohydrates, having them choose from each group means that they are combining these two foods themselves. Even if they are not always accustomed to the foods they have picked, they have some control over their own meal.

A great way to implement this every single day is to have designated boxes for school lunches in the fridge. Have carbohydrates, protein, fruit and vegetables separated. Then simply ask your child to choose what they would like from each section, making sure they select a different item every day to avoid food jagging (page 36).

Communication is key, so chatting with your child about their favourite foods can potentially inspire a host of tasty lunchbox ideas. For example, was there ever a particular sauce or soup they had that they really liked? If so, plan to recreate it for them. My girls adore pesto, as do many children, so I am always thinking up new ways to add in new veggies. So far, I have created versions using basil, pistachio, kale and courgette (page 158) and they are a hit every time!

If you are cooking for your child's lunch, don't be afraid to get them involved. I am a huge advocate of having your children in the kitchen. The process of preparing food familiarises them with flavours, textures and smells that may otherwise have made them cautious. Children who have played a part in creating a meal are almost always more likely to eat it. Not only will they find the activity fun, but they will bring their lunch to school with a sense of pride and excitement.

Engaging the Senses

Our senses have a huge impact on what we do and don't want to eat. I am sure that something that looks delicious and smells amazing excites you more than something that doesn't - and children are the same. Less sensory meals may be just as tasty, but meals that engage your senses are the ones that will appeal to you most and you will remember and crave time and time again.

When considering what goes in your child's lunchbox it's important to understand and consider all of their senses. Your five senses work together to help your brain understand and react to your environment. Therefore, any overwhelming or negative senses can cause your child to reject their meal. It can also put them off trying something similar in the future.

Sight

The sense of sight is the first we engage so it can be the biggest barrier to a child eating their lunch. When packing your child's lunchbox, always think about what their reaction will be when they open it and see what is inside.

Tips to make your child's lunch look more appealing:

- Show your child what's going into their lunchbox. Alert them to any unfavourable foods as it's crucial not to surprise them with something they may not like.
- Allow them to pack their own lunchbox and they will be sure to eat it all. Make sure they select at least one item from each food group; carbohydrate, protein, fruit and/or vegetables (see page 18).
- Separate 'comfortable' and 'uncomfortable' foods into different containers.
- Change up the way you offer food each time e.g. cubes of cheese vs. grated cheese.
- Add a colourful dip like salsa for tortillas (page 163) or pesto for carrot sticks (page 157).

Smell

Smell can be powerful in triggering emotions and memories of meals you've had in the past. It also has a large impact on our sense of taste and can improve or inhibit the way we taste things! Ever notice how when you have a blocked nose from a cold you can't taste things properly?

You therefore want to ensure that when your child opens their lunchbox they are met with pleasant or neutral smells that enable them to explore each element of their meal. Be aware of strong smells from foods like egg and tuna which can be overpowering. This is where placing different food in separate containers really comes into play. By doing so any strong smells can be concealed.

Try my Tuna and Sweetcorn Sandwich (page 126) but make sure to lock it in an airtight container!

Taste

Even if you make the most appealing lunchbox, if it doesn't taste good then there is little chance your child will finish their meal.

When weaning a baby, I advise parents to taste every purée or meal they serve up. If you don't think what you have made tastes good it is very likely your child will feel the same. And remember, texture is just as important. Trying what is going into your child's lunchbox will really help you understand why your child may reject a particular food. It might be that it needs a quick and easy adjustment to make it taste better or it may be a question of: Is the bread stale? Have you made muffins so low in sugar that they now taste bland? Having two school going daughters myself I have made sure that every recipe in this book has been taste tested by them both.

Taste test my Cheese Scones (page 85) for an alternative to a sandwich.

Sound

Children not only like the way something crunches in their mouth but the sound it makes as they bite into it. They may explore this sound by opening their mouth while they bite down on it or moving their jaw in different directions. Whatever they do if it is highly sensory pleasing, in no time they will have eaten it all!

Try my Carrot and Lentil Soup with crunchy croutons (page 72).

Touch

Children learn and explore objects through touch. Even as adults we still reach out and touch something new to help categorise it in our brain. This is why it's so important to get your child in the kitchen to help prepare their food. Exposure to what's going in their lunchbox will increase their willingness to taste new foods and make it easier to increase the variety you offer.

My Apple and Banana Muffins (page 92) have a great texture and are perfect for little hands.

Checklist

- ☐ Is the food separated into different containers to manage smells, prevent contamination of tastes, promote freshness and make things interesting?
- ☐ Are the contents visually appealing and colourful?
- ☐ Is the smell inviting?
- ☐ Is the texture appealing for them to reach in and touch it? Do you have a variety of textures?
- ☐ Most importantly, does it taste good?

When Your Child Doesn't Finish Their Lunchbox

Starting out in big school

Moving to big school is a huge transition for both you and your little one. Most likely, your child just graduated from the cosy atmosphere of a crèche. Here, one childcare worker is usually assigned to three or four children, and the food is a soft, mushy dinner like a casserole or shepherd's pie. With lots of attention from the surrounding adults and some peer pressure from their friends, your child probably gobbled up their dinner, leaving you with nothing to worry about.

This is why the sudden change in routine when they begin big school can be daunting for parents and children alike. Suddenly, your little one has to be responsible for and manage their own meal-time. They have to take out their lunchbox, eat all their food and then put away their lunchbox - all by themselves. Although it sounds straightforward, it can actually be quite difficult for many children to grasp the concept of what a school lunch is. They may not even understand how their packed lunch is supposed to be eaten or when they should have their snack.

You may be left feeling a little hopeless when your child comes home with their lunchbox almost as full as when they left. In this new environment children just do not understand how to allocate time for eating. While this is understandable, you must explain to them that it is important to eat. Breaking down the food groups and explaining why each one is so important will help them to understand why food is necessary. During their first year at school, both of my girls eventually learned how to eat their lunch during the allotted time. It simply just takes time.

All in all, don't be too worried if your child initially doesn't eat all of their lunch. If possible, try to encourage them to make sure they finish it when they get home and before they eat their afternoon snack. Keep encouraging them, making sure that they understand when each aspect of their lunch-box should be eaten. Eventually, they will fall into a comfortable school routine, and they'll return home everyday with all their food eaten.

Older Children

It can be trickier to solve the problem of older children not eating their lunch. In this case, they are used to the school routine so over-stimulation will not be the issue. Instead, it is most likely picky eating. Check out page 36 for more ways to get your child to eat a wider variety of foods.

The best way to ensure your child eats their lunch is to let them choose the contents themselves. Getting your children involved in the kitchen is a fantastic way to make them more comfortable around food. This has to be within reason of course. Make sure that they understand the food groups and choose something from each category. Having a voice in what they will be eating means that there will be no surprises come lunch time. The food will be far more appealing if they have picked it out themselves instead of it being forced upon them.

Most importantly, I always ensure that my two girls are eating their lunch by checking their lunch bag every day when they come home from school. If they haven't, they must sit down and finish it before they get a snack or embark on a new activity. I want them to understand that there is a consequence to not eating their lunch at school. By eating their lunch they will be able to concentrate better and be able to muster enough energy for after school activities. It's crucial to do the same with their water bottles too. Children need to continuously drink water even more than adults to avoid dehydration as they have more active lifestyles.

After School Snacking

If my girls return home with their lunch finished, I always offer them a snack. This could be a savoury muffin, some wholemeal toast or perhaps a yoghurt. For some families, the afternoon is actually the time that they find best to serve their children dinner. Their little ones might be at their most hungry and most receptive to trying new foods. It is perfectly fine if this is the method that suits your family's routine. Otherwise, I would suggest that having a heavier meal in the evening is best.

If you decide to eat later, I recommend providing a snack first to curb after-school cravings. Then leave a gap of about three hours between this and dinner so that they are guaranteed to feel hungry again. Eating dinner later when everyone is around means that you can sit around the table as a family and talk. This quality time is so special! Engaging with your child and having them open up about their day means that you may potentially pick up on important issues or struggles at school, as well as hearing about the fun stuff they are doing! Moments like this can be missed when a family does not eat together. It is also the best way of encouraging children to eat a wider variety of foods and the same foods that you are eating.

Tips for afternoon snacks:

- Ensure your child's lunchbox is fully eaten and water is drank before offering an afternoon snack. If their lunch isn't finished encourage them to eat this first.
- Choose foods that are different to their morning snack but try to include a carbohydrate, protein, fruit and/or vegetable.
- If you have more time in the afternoon you can whip up some delicious pancakes and top them with lots of fruit.
- Have a cut off time for snacks to make sure you have at least a 3 hour gap between snacks and dinner.
- If choosing shop bought options ensure they are low in salt and sugar (see reading food labels on page 38).

Check out my snacks recipes from page 185.

Encouraging Your 'Picky' Child to Try New Foods

We would all love to have our children eat every food that's on offer but this is usually not always the case. As a busy parent, it can be frustrating trying to keep up with ever-changing likes and dislikes. So in order to include variety you need to keep including new foods in your child's lunchbox.

The following strategies for offering new foods for children, picky or not, will help you include new foods and get your child eating a more varied lunchbox.

Give your child control

Encourage your child to help choose what goes in their lunch and they'll be more likely to eat it (see page 26 on including your child in making their lunch).

Offer a variety of foods

By pairing 'comfortable' preferred foods with 'uncomfortable' less favoured foods your child will feel less anxious and be more likely to give new foods a try! As I have talked about before it's important to encourage your child to choose from each food group and to add variety each day.

Avoid offering the same foods again and again (food jagging)

Try to have at least a two day gap before you offer the same foods again in the same format. By providing the exact same food over and over again you can cause food jagging. This is when your child eventually gets burnt out by certain foods and will no longer want to eat them.

Separate foods

Use individual pots for the different elements of your child's lunch such as sandwiches, snacks, dips etc. Avoid a lunchbox with compartments that don't have seperate covers. Juices from foods like fruit can easily run across to things like sandwiches making them soggy and undesirable. Even worse, 'comfortable' and 'uncomfortable' foods may end up touching which can be a 'picky' child's worst nightmare!

Use vegetable alternatives

It's not easy getting vegetables into lunches, especially if your child isn't a fan of them. A great way to increase your child's veggie intake is by making delicious vegetable spreads like my Basil and Courgette Pesto (page 158).

Batch cook

Stock your freezer with homemade healthy options for meals and snacks. Recipes like my Apple and Banana Muffins (page 92) and Quick Bolognese (page 137) are perfect to batch cook. Read more about batch cooking on page 14.

Recreate favourites

There are bound to be restaurant meals or shop bought snacks that your child loves and will eat without any trouble. Recreate nutritious home-made versions. For example, most children enjoy popcorn at the movies which can often be too salty or sweet. Make your own flavours with my recipes on page 187; you can even pack some as a treat in your child's lunchbox.

Use an assortment of colour

Children love colour. A colourful lunchbox built on a variety of foods will be more appealing.

Give second chances

Encourage your child to eat any untouched food when they return home. Praise them for finishing anything but never force them.

Never give up

Most importantly, keep trying and never give up! Your child will gradually increase the variety of foods they will eat. Patience is key.

#TryItTuesday

At first it may be difficult to broaden the range of foods your child eats. Start off by introducing one new food each week. In our house, we call it 'Try it Tuesday' as every Tuesday I serve up something new yet familiar to my girls. Follow my Mummy Cooks Instagram (@MummyCooks) for inspiration on what to try. I'd love to also follow your journey so tag your posts with **#TryItTuesday** to share your photos with me.

Reading Food Labels

For the most part if you are making up your child's lunchbox from scratch and using the recipes from my Mummy Cooks books you won't have to worry about sugar and salt content. However, with the best will in the world there is going to be shop bought snacks, cereals and drinks included in your child's diet. This is perfectly fine as long as you are aware of labelling.

Concentrate on sugars and salts and read per 100g rather than per biscuit or slice. A lot of foods that are low in sugar are actually quite high in salt, so it's important to keep an eye out. Sneaky tricks like this can make something seemingly nutritious actually quite unhealthy.

Foods	Sugar	Salt
High	Over 22.5g	Over 1.5g
Medium	Between 5g and 22.5g	Between 0.3g and 1.5g
Low	5g and below	0.3g and below

Source: Diabetes Ireland www.diabetes.ie

Yoghurt

Yoghurt is a fantastic lunchbox snack but like everything should be given in moderation. Yoghurt offers several health benefits including protein, calcium and probiotics. Natural yoghurt is the best option and has little or no sugar. You can also always serve it with a fruit purée for added flavour.

Check out my Yoghurt Fruit Dips on page 188 for some homemade versions. If this it out of the question for your child who is used to sweetened yoghurt, just be knowledgeable when purchasing. Generally, you should be looking for foods that contain less than 5g of sugar per 100g. In a yoghurt that contains fruit this number will usually be upwards of 10g per 100g, so it's important that you only offer it once per day.

Cheese

Cheese provides calcium needed for healthy bones and teeth. Most children love cheese and it can be a handy sandwich filler or snack. Cheese can be high in salt so always offer in moderation. As with most foods, the more natural varieties you buy, the better. It's an easy temptation to get products aimed at children, such as string cheeses. A lot of these don't really taste like the real deal, which gives your child a false idea of what cheese should be. As a result, they will be less likely to eat healthier natural cheeses later on because they won't be accustomed to the taste.

Portion Sizes

Milk, Yoghurt and Cheese

Children up to 8 years old should be offered up to 3 portions per day. At 9 years through to the teenage years this increases to 5 portions.

For cheese use two thumbs, width and depth to guide serving size.

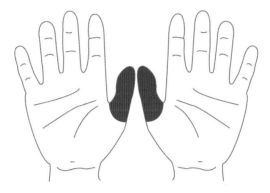

Adapted from Food Pyramid www.safefood.eu

Stocking Your Freezer

I have to admit, I have a little bit of an obsession with my freezer. I purchased the biggest one I could get for my kitchen and it has definitely paid off. All my food inside is so valuable (especially in terms of effort) that I have the greatest fear of power cuts. If you have room for a larger or second freezer, go for it! It'll pay for itself in the amount of time you save through the weeks and you'll be able to stock up enough meals to stop you from resorting to unhealthier shop bought options or takeaways on busy days.

How to freeze food safely

Try to consume frozen food within 3-4 months. Remember to only place cold food in your freezer. See the diagram below for steps on safely storing your food. A good way to make sure you use up your batch cooking is to label and place more recently cooked foods towards the back and older food at the front.

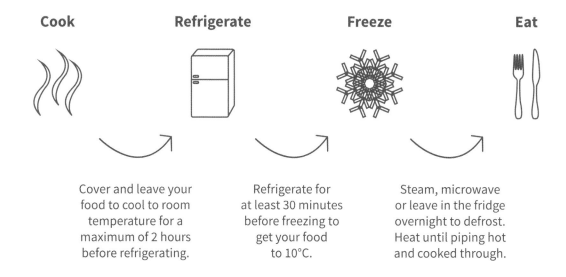

Cook	**Refrigerate**	**Freeze**	**Eat**
	Cover and leave your food to cool to room temperature for a maximum of 2 hours before refrigerating.	Refrigerate for at least 30 minutes before freezing to get your food to 10°C.	Steam, microwave or leave in the fridge overnight to defrost. Heat until piping hot and cooked through.

Foods that are perfect to freeze:

Fruit

Frozen fruit is so readily available and perfect for quickly whipping up a healthy smoothie (check out my Smoothie recipes from page 203). It's a great option when certain fruits are out of season and you can even take advantage of seasonal fruit on offer by washing, chopping and freezing some yourself. Bananas that are overripe can be frozen whole and later used in baking like my Banana Bread on page 101.

Vegetables

Perfect for when you run out of fresh produce; stir some straight into curries or stews. Frozen peas are a staple in our house as they work great in almost everything.

Muffins

Place in resealable food storage bags and then when you need one remove it. Defrost in the fridge overnight or in a microwave using the defrost setting. Great to have on hand for breakfast on the go or a lunchbox snack. Check out my Ham and Cheese Muffins on page 93.

Sauces

Recipes like my Quick Bolognese (page 137) and my Marinara sauce (page 148) are ideal to freeze. Stir some through pasta and place in a heated food flask for a quick and easy hot lunch.

Pestos & Spreads

These freeze really well. Just make sure to defrost overnight in the fridge. Perfect to make sandwiches more nutritious and exciting. They are also great for sending in as dips. Check out my Pesto and Spreads recipes from page 157.

Soups

Make up a batch of soup and store in portion pots and freeze for future use. Simply defrost overnight in the fridge then heat through and add to your child's food flask. Check out my Soup recipes from page 65.

Herbs & Spices

Did you know you can freeze almost everything including leftover herbs and spices? I usually freeze ginger which can be grated into dishes and herbs like mint and coriander which can be stirred straight in. (Note: Frozen herbs work perfectly as an ingredient but become soggy when defrosted so aren't suitable as a garnish).

Homemade Chicken & Fish Nuggets

Breadcrumb strips of chicken or fish to have ready for the perfect Friday night fakeaway! Freeze raw then cook in the oven, straight from frozen, until piping hot and cooked through.

Make sure to invest in enough BPA free storage pots in different portion sizes to do large batch cooks.

Check out MummyCooks.com for our full range of portion pots.

Lunchbox Schedule

WEEK 1	SMALL BREAK	LUNCH BREAK	LUNCH BREAK FRUIT	AFTERNOON SNACK
MONDAY	Almond Butter Balls (page 200)	Smoked Salmon & Cream Cheese Pinwheels (page 121)	Orange Segments	Potato & Carrot Waffles (page 182)
TUESDAY	Stick of Pepper & Hummus Dip (page 167)	Leftover Dinner: Quick Bolognese (page 137)	Grapes	Roasted Sweet Chickpeas (page 195)
WEDNESDAY	Blueberry Bread (page 102)	Curried Parsnip & Pear Soup (page 78)	Apple	Vegetable Egg Muffins (page 89)
THURSDAY	Buttered Popcorn (page 187)	Chicken Quesadilla (page 123)	Pineapple	Banana Bread (page 101)
FRIDAY	Sweetcorn Pancakes (page 177)	Basil & Courgette Pasta (page 158)	Cherries	Cheese Biscuits (page 189)

SMALL BREAK	LUNCH BREAK	LUNCH BREAK FRUIT	AFTERNOON SNACK	WEEK 2	
Vegetable Crisps (page 190)	Roasted Red Pepper & Sweetcorn Pasta (page 107)	Pear	Apple Cinnamon Waffles (page 181)		MONDAY
Orange Greek Yoghurt Fruit Dip with Rice Cakes (page 188)	Tuna & Sweetcorn Sandwich (page 126)	Banana	Healthy Granola Bars (page 197)		TUESDAY
Dough Balls (page 95)	Leftover Dinner: Cauliflower Macaroni & Cheese (page 147)	Strawberries	Apple & Blueberry Oat Muffins (page 91)		WEDNESDAY
Cheese Scones (page 85)	Chicken & Avocado Focaccia (page 131)	Plum	Carrot & Orange Smoothie (page 208)		THURSDAY
Trail Mix (page 198)	Pasta & Alfredo Sauce (page 153)	Peach	Banana & Chocolate Breakfast Cookie (page 61)		FRIDAY

How to Use This Book

The basic principle of this book is that all recipes are child-friendly and easy to prepare. Each recipe has a portion guide and has symbols to show if it contains any allergens.

Portion Sizes

Check out my lunchbox checklist for portion pot sizes on page 16. Each recipe is by adult portion or per slice/muffin. An adult portion is equal to two child portions.

Allergens and Substitutes

If a recipe contains any of the following allergens, it will be indicated with the symbols shown below. With so many children with allergies it's important that we respect any bans on foods in the classroom. I've therefore suggested alternatives whether for your child or to consider the safety of others.

Gluten

Substitute flours for coconut, almond or rice flour. Gluten free flour is also available as well as gluten free pastas. In this recipe book I have included oats as a gluten free food. Some off the shelf oats can be contaminated with gluten so if your child is a coeliac you need to source certified gluten free oats.

⏀ Dairy

For milk, use alternatives like coconut, almond or oat milk. Dairy free margarines, creams and even cheeses can also be found in many shops. I have included full fat milk in all my recipes as this is what I use for my children who lead a very active lifestyle and have a healthy diet. You can substitute if you have been advised to use reduced fat milk by a health professional.

Nuts

For many recipes like pestos and nut butters, substitute nuts with seeds like pumpkin or sunflower seeds. Experiment with different seed varieties to find one that you love best.

⬭ Eggs

When cooking, substitute every egg for 1 tbsp of ground flaxseed mixed with 2 ½ tbsp of water. Leave the mixture to sit for 5 minutes to thicken before using.

Breakfast on the Go

Some children are just not hungry in the morning and it's a battle to get them to eat. There are also times when it's simply not manageable to make breakfast in the morning. These recipes allow you to have breakfast ready to eat with no morning prep, pack a healthy breakfast for your child's snack time or have something to enjoy on the go.

Nut-Free Granola

I always have a batch of Granola stored away in my cupboard as it's perfect to have to hand for a fulfilling breakfast or lunchbox snack. Many schools have put a ban on nuts altogether, which is why my nut-free version is perfect to send in. Serving up Granola with yoghurt is a great way to get children who aren't a fan of yoghurt to give it a go - they'll love the crunchy texture and added flavour from the cinnamon and vanilla. Just make sure to pack the Granola separately and allow your child to add it as a topping so it doesn't go soggy.

Makes: 6 Adult Portions

2 tbsp butter or coconut oil
8 tbsp honey/maple syrup
1 tsp vanilla extract
180g porridge oats
120g wholemeal flour
2 tsp baking powder
1 tsp cinnamon
1 tsp salt
35g sunflower seeds
35g pumpkin seeds

1. Preheat the oven to 180°C and line a baking tray with parchment paper.

2. Place the butter or coconut oil in a small saucepan over a low heat until melted. Add in the honey or maple syrup and vanilla extract. Stir over a low heat until combined, then remove from the heat.

3. Combine all of the dry ingredients in a large bowl.

4. Stir in the wet ingredients and mix so that all of the dry ingredients are well coated.

5. Bake in the oven for 15-20 minutes, until golden brown. Remove from the oven and allow to cool fully before storing in an airtight container.

Overnight Berry & Chia Seed Oats

Overnight oats are definitely a take on the traditional Bircher muesli. But instead of yoghurt I like to add milk. Since overnight oats require no cooking they are perfect when you are in a rush getting the children ready in the morning. Allow your child to make up their pot of oats, encouraging them to add lots of seeds and fruit.

Makes: 1 Adult Portion

240ml full fat milk
60g porridge oats
30g mixed frozen berries
1 tbsp chia seeds
1 tbsp chopped nuts

To serve:
1 tsp maple syrup or honey
Fresh berries

Tip: Overnight oats are the perfect option for when you have an early flight. Because there is no liquid you will easily get them through security.

1. Add all of your ingredients to a bowl, mix to combine. Cover and leave overnight.

2. In the morning serve with some fresh berries and syrup.

Bircher Muesli

This traditional Swiss muesli is great to make up the night before and have either as breakfast on the go or if your child isn't so good with breakfast as a mid-morning snack at school.

Makes: 1 Adult Portion

2 tbsp porridge oats
30ml apple juice
1 tbsp mixed berries
½ banana
1 tbsp natural yoghurt

To serve:
Seeds of your choice
Fresh berries

1. In a bowl add your porridge oats and apple juice. Allow to soak before adding in your berries and banana. Mash the berries and the banana in and then add your yoghurt.

2. Cover and place in your fridge overnight. Serve topped with fresh berries and seeds.

Vegetable Omelette

When I get asked about what to put in a child's food flask I always mention an omelette. It's not something you imagine when you think of a lunchbox but with a warm flask it is a great nutritious option. Grating in the courgette will make your child more accepting of it and you can mix things up and use any vegetables your child might enjoy.

Makes: 1 Child Portion

Olive oil
1 tbsp grated courgette
1 egg
1 tbsp sweetcorn
Salt and pepper

Tip: Omelettes work well with salads such as my Fruity Couscous on page 114.

1. Heat the oil in a small frying pan over a medium heat.

2. Add the grated courgette to the pan. Sauté for 2 minutes until softened.

3. Meanwhile, crack the egg into a small bowl. Add the sweetcorn and whisk with a fork. Season with salt and pepper.

4. Once the courgette is soft, add the egg mix to the courgette. Leave to cook for 2 minutes.

5. Carefully flip the egg using a spatula. Cook for another minute until golden.

6. Transfer to a plate and serve. Alternatively serve warm in your child's food flask.

Banana French Toast

Delicious eggy banana toast - this recipe can easily be made up the night before and then reheated on a dry pan.

Makes: 1 Portion

Olive oil
A small knob of butter
½ banana, mashed
1 egg
1 tbsp full fat milk
A dash of vanilla extract
1 slice wholemeal bread

To serve:
½ banana
Sprinkle cinnamon

1. Place a frying pan over a medium heat. Add the olive oil and butter.

2. Whisk the banana and egg in a bowl. Add the milk and vanilla extract and combine.

3. Pick the bread up with a fork and dip the back and front in the egg mixture.

4. Transfer to the pan. Fry for a minute on either side until golden brown.

5. Serve topped with banana slices and cinnamon.

Nut Butter & Chia Seed Toast

When time is tight there is nothing easier than a slice of toast. Make it a meal by adding some nut butter, chia seeds and sliced banana.

Makes: 1 Child Portion

1 slice wholemeal bread
1 tbsp nut butter (pg 173)
½ banana, sliced
½ tsp chia seeds

Tip: Freeze your bread so that you always have some on hand to make up this quick and easy snack.

1. Toast your bread and spread the nut butter over it.

2. Top with sliced banana and chia seeds. Serve straight away.

Fruit Wraps

A super easy breakfast that can be made up in a few minutes and taken with you on the go. Let your child choose their favourite fruits to go inside.

Makes: 1 Wrap

1 tbsp yoghurt or cream cheese
1 wholemeal tortilla wrap
3 strawberries, cut in half
Handful of blueberries

Tip: Wraps can go soggy in a lunchbox so it's best to leave out the fruit and let your child put it together when they are ready to eat.

1. Spread a layer of the yoghurt or cream cheese onto the wrap. Top with fruit and roll it up.

2. Serve as is or cut in half to make it more manageable for your child.

Cinnamon Breakfast Energy Balls

Energy balls are great for breakfast on the go or as an afternoon snack. If you want to make them nut-free swap the nut butter for pumpkin or sunflower seed butter.

Makes: 12 Balls

1 tbsp cinnamon
140g porridge oats
250g nut butter (pg 173)
4 tbsp honey
75g desiccated coconut
80g ground flaxseed
1 tsp vanilla extract

1. Put all the ingredients into your food processor and blend until combined.

2. Remove the mixture from the food processor and shape into bite sized balls.

3. Store in airtight portion pots for up to one week or freeze for future use.

Banana & Chocolate Breakfast Cookies

Love these cookies - what a treat! I have replaced the usual butter with bananas to make them extra nutritious and lovely and moist. Swap out the nut butter for a nut-free version and pack them in your child's lunchbox for the perfect breakfast on the go or snack.

Makes: 18 Mini Cookies

45g porridge oats
1 medium banana, mashed
65g of cashew butter (pg 173)
½ tsp vanilla extract
Pinch of salt
2 tbsp chocolate chips
2½ tbsp raisins or dried cranberries
1 tbsp of maple syrup
1 tbsp desiccated coconut

1. Preheat the oven to 180°C. Line a baking tray with parchment paper.

2. In a bowl add all the ingredients mixing until combined.

3. Shape into cookies and place on your baking tray. Use the palm of your hand to gently press down the cookies, as they do not spread during baking.

4. Bake for 15 minutes and remove to a cooling rack.

5. Store in an airtight container for up to a week.

Messy Jessie Cereal Bars

My youngest Jessica came up with this recipe, oh and the title! We love that these are nut-free so the girls can have one in their lunchbox on treat Friday. They also require zero cooking which is always great.

Makes: 12 Bars

135g porridge oats
30g puffed rice cereal
2 tbsp flaxseed
50g desiccated coconut
100g chocolate chips
100g honey or maple syrup
85g coconut oil
2 tsp vanilla extract
¼ tsp salt

1. In a large bowl combine your dry ingredients.

2. Melt the honey or maple syrup and coconut oil in a saucepan over a medium heat until combined. Add in your vanilla extract and salt.

3. Pour the wet ingredients into your dry, making sure the dry ingredients are well coated.

4. Transfer the mixture onto a baking tray lined with parchment paper and press down.

5. Refrigerate overnight or for at least 6 hours.

6. Remove from the fridge and cut into bars either square or rectangular. Wrap individually and place back in your fridge or freezer for future use.

Soups

Soups make such a wholesome, nutritious meal. You can really play around with flavours, textures and seasonal fruits and vegetables. You can even mimic the flavours and tastes of your family's favourite meals. If for example your child likes chicken curry, create a soup with spices and curried vegetables. If they like sweeter tastes, use naturally sweet vegetables.

If your child isn't the biggest fan of the smooth consistency of soup, remember you can serve it chunkier to suit their tastes. A side of crusty bread also works great as it adds that extra texture and substance that can convert the pickiest of eaters. To serve a soup as a warm school lunch be sure to grab one of my Mummy Cooks food flasks.

Sweet Potato & Carrot Soup

This deliciously sweet soup is so warming and satisfying on a chilly day. Simply freeze and defrost as needed to make meals stress-free. Team this up with some of my focaccia bread on page 98 and you will be in the good books for the week!

Makes: 4 Adult Portions

400g sweet potato, peeled and cubed
300g carrots, peeled and chopped
3 cloves of garlic
3 tbsp olive oil
Salt to taste
1 onion, finely chopped
1 tsp cumin
1 tsp ground ginger
650ml low salt vegetable stock
200ml coconut milk

Tip: If your child isn't a fan of soup, serving it with chunky bread will encourage them to give it a try.

1. Preheat the oven to 200°C.

2. Place the vegetables on a roasting tin, leaving the garlic cloves whole. Drizzle with 1 tbsp olive oil and season with salt. Roast for about 35-40 minutes.

3. Meanwhile, heat the remaining oil in a large saucepan over a medium heat. Add the onion, cumin and ginger and sauté for a few minutes until the onion is translucent.

4. After a few minutes pour in the stock. When the vegetables are roasted take them out of the oven and add to the saucepan. Make sure to squeeze the garlic cloves out of their skins and discard the skin. Simmer for about 10 minutes.

5. Remove from the heat and blend to the desired consistency. Stir in the coconut milk and serve.

Pea & Mint Soup

A true classic, I have fond memories eating this soup as a child. Although I always serve it warm, this soup is particularly nice served cold in the summer months when we have fresh mint in the garden.

Makes: 4 Adult Portions

1 tbsp olive oil
1 large leek, finely chopped
1 celery stalk, finely chopped
1 bay leaf
4 tbsp mint, finely chopped
2 potatoes, peeled and cubed
800ml low salt vegetable stock
250g peas, frozen
120ml full fat milk
Salt and pepper

1. Heat the olive oil in a large saucepan over a medium heat. Cook the leek for about 5 minutes until softened.

2. Add in the celery, bay leaf, mint and potatoes and cook for 3 minutes with the lid ajar.

3. Add the stock and bring the mixture to the boil. Reduce the heat and simmer with the lid on for 20 minutes. Add the peas and cook for a further 5 minutes.

4. Once the vegetables are nice and tender, remove the bay leaf and blend everything together before stirring in the milk. Season with salt and pepper to taste.

5. Serve straight away with some crusty bread or store for future use.

Hearty Vegetable Soup

As much as I love experimenting with new flavours of soups for my girls, I always come back to this simple vegetable soup recipe. Soup is a great way of using up any leftover vegetables, so change it up depending on what you have in stock.

Makes: 4 Adult Portions

1 tbsp olive oil
4 celery stalks, chopped
2 onions, chopped
4 carrots, peeled and chopped
1 litre low salt vegetable or chicken stock
1 tsp oregano
1 tsp ground coriander
1 tsp dried parsley

To serve:
Crème fraiche (optional)

Tip: Soups are great for a fussy eater, just make sure to pick a soup that is a colour of foods they are most accepting of.

1. Heat the olive oil in a large saucepan over a medium heat. Add the vegetables and cook for 4-5 minutes, until the onion starts to become translucent.

2. Add the stock and the herbs.

3. Bring the mixture to the boil before reducing to a simmer for 30-40 minutes until the vegetables are cooked through.

4. Transfer the soup to your blender and blitz until smooth and creamy.

5. Serve with a dollop of crème fraiche and enjoy.

Carrot & Lentil Soup

Lentils are a good source of fiber, which boosts your child's digestive health. They also contain iron, zinc and potassium - amazing! Lentils can be unappealing on their own but the addition of the sweet carrots in this recipe should encourage even the fussiest of eaters to give it a try. I have been making this soup since my girls were babies and it's now a firm favourite when the cold weather kicks in.

Makes: 4 Adult portions

2 tbsp olive oil
1 onion, chopped
1 clove of garlic, finely chopped
2 celery stalks, chopped
4 large carrots, peeled and chopped
75g red split lentils, soaked and washed
500ml low salt chicken or vegetable stock

To serve:
1 slice of wholemeal bread (optional)

Tip: Place the croutons in a separate container so they stay nice and crunchy for your child to add them to their soup.

1. Heat 1 tbsp of the olive oil in a large saucepan over a medium heat. Cook the onion, garlic, celery and carrots for 6-8 minutes, until the onions start to soften.

2. Add in the lentils and the stock and bring the mixture to the boil. Reduce the heat and simmer with the lid on for 20-25 minutes.

3. Once the vegetables are nice and tender, blend everything together to the desired consistency.

4. To make croutons, slice the bread into cubes and heat the remaining tbsp of olive oil in a frying pan. Toast the croutons for 2-3 minutes on each side until golden and brown. Place on top of your soup and enjoy!

Chicken Noodle Soup

This chicken noodle soup is the ultimate comfort food. There may be a little prep involved but it's definitely worth the effort and it freezes really well. If you don't have a spiraliser handy just use a peeler. Heat through in the morning before school and pop into your child's preheated food flask.

Makes: 4 Adult Portions

For the broth:
4 chicken thighs, skinned, bone in
2 carrots, chopped
1 small onion, chopped
2 celery stalks, chopped
1 handful of fresh parsley
1 handful of fresh thyme
Salt and pepper

Noodles:
1 carrot, spiralised
2 x 150g Udon noodles
1 courgette, spiralised
Small handful of fresh coriander
to garnish

1. Add all of the broth ingredients except the salt and pepper to a large saucepan and fill with water until everything is covered.

2. Bring to the boil over a high heat, reduce the heat and simmer for 30-40 minutes with the lid on, until the chicken has cooked through.

3. Remove the chicken and set aside, before straining the remainder of the mixture and discarding the vegetables and herbs.

4. Bring the broth to the boil and simmer for a further 5-10 minutes to enhance the flavour. Add salt and pepper to taste.

5. Once you are ready to serve your soup, tear the chicken away from the bones, add into the broth with the spiralised carrot and noodles and simmer for 5 minutes.

6. Turn off the hob, add the spiralised courgette. Leave to stand for 3-5 minutes with the lid on. Garnish with coriander and serve.

Chicken Soup

Pure soul food, this hearty chicken soup is the perfect pick-me-up when your child is feeling under the weather or you just simply want to send them to school with a warm nourishing meal. This soup freezes well so make sure to make plenty of extra portions for a quick and easy lunch.

Makes: 4 Adult Portions

2 skinless chicken breasts
2 carrots, peeled and chopped
2 celery stalks, chopped
2 small onions, finely chopped
1 litre low salt chicken stock
½ tsp freshly ground black pepper
1 tsp fresh or dried parsley
1 tsp fresh or dried thyme

Tip: Remember to portion soup before freezing so you can reheat the correct amount needed for your child's school lunch.

1. Place a large pot over medium heat. Add all of the ingredients and bring to the boil.

2. Reduce heat, cover and simmer for 30-40 minutes.

3. When the chicken is cooked through and the vegetables are soft when pierced with a fork, transfer to a food processor and blitz until smooth.

4. Serve warm and top with a sprinkle of fresh black pepper to taste.

Gazpacho

Gazpacho is a cold nutritious soup made with raw vegetables. It's super easy to make, you might even have time in the morning before school. This recipe is so light and refreshing, I can guarantee your child will love it. Just place in your pre-chilled flask for a light and refreshing lunch option.

Makes: 4 Adult Portions

1 tin of chopped tomatoes
1 red pepper, roughly chopped
1 small onion, roughly chopped
2 cloves of garlic
10 basil leaves
½ a cucumber
1 tbsp olive oil

1. Put the tomatoes, pepper, onion, garlic, basil and cucumber into a food processor and blend until smooth.

2. Add in the olive oil and mix until just combined.

3. Serve straight away or place in your pre-chilled food flask.

Tip: Gazpacho can also be served like an aperitif, in fun glasses with a colored straw.

Curried Parsnip & Pear Soup

This sweet and savoury combination is delicious. The natural sweetness from the parsnips and pear will make your child more receptive to new flavours, so don't be afraid to give it a go. Pears and parsnips are in their prime in the autumn and winter months so this soup is perfect during colder days.

Makes: 4 Adult Portions

25g unsalted butter
1 tbsp olive oil
1 onion, finely chopped
1 clove of garlic, minced
1 medium potato, peeled and chopped
600g parsnips, peeled and chopped
1 tsp mild curry powder
1 litre low salt vegetable stock
300ml full fat milk
1 ripe pear, peeled, cored and chopped

1. Heat the butter and oil in a large saucepan over a medium heat.

2. Cook the onions and garlic until soft.

3. Add the potato, parsnip and curry powder and cook for a further 1-2 minutes.

4. Add the stock, milk and pear and bring to the boil.

5. Reduce the heat to a simmer with the lid on for 20-25 minutes.

6. Once the parsnips are nice and tender, blend everything together in a food processor.

7. Serve straight away with some crusty bread or store for future use.

Curried Cauliflower & Cheese Soup

One of our favourite activities as a family is to go on hikes. Last year we did a hike around Glendalough and on our return we visited a cafe that served some curried cauliflower soup. The girls didn't stop talking about how delicious it was. I just had to recreate it and we added the cheese part. If you are not so fond of the curried flavour then it's equally as tasty without.

Makes: 6 Adult Portions

1 tbsp unsalted butter
1 large onion, finely chopped
1 large cauliflower, cut into florets
1 potato, peeled and chopped
½ tsp mild curry powder
700ml low salt vegetable stock
400ml full fat milk
100g Cheddar cheese, grated
Salt and pepper

1. Heat the butter in a large saucepan over a medium heat, then cook the onion for about 5 minutes.

2. Add the cauliflower, potato and curry powder, stir and cook gently for 5 minutes.

3. Pour in the stock and bring to the boil. Reduce the heat, mix in the milk and simmer with a lid partially on for 10-15 minutes.

4. Once the cauliflower and potato is tender, blend everything together.

5. Return back to the saucepan and gently heat to a simmer. Add your cheese and stir until melted and mixed in. Add more stock or water if your soup is too thick. Season with salt and pepper to taste.

SOUPS

Curried Butternut Squash Soup

This recipe is courtesy of a friend Paddy who made this soup for us when visiting. My daughter who is big into her curried soups begged me to make it when we got home. I followed up and asked for the recipe and couldn't believe it was so simple. Ashleigh now makes this for herself because according to her it needs exactly the right amount of curry powder and lemon juice. So please do adjust the recipe according to your preferences.

Makes: 4 Adult portions

1 butternut squash
Low salt vegetable stock (enough to cover)
Squeeze of lemon juice
½ tsp mild curry powder
Salt and pepper

1. Peel, de-seed and cube the butternut squash.

2. Place the cubed squash into a small saucepan and add enough stock to just cover everything.

3. Bring to a simmer and cook uncovered for 20 minutes or until the butternut squash is soft.

4. When cooked, transfer to a blender and blend until you get a creamy and smooth texture. Add more of the stock if the soup is too thick for your liking.

5. Squeeze in some lemon juice and add the curry powder. At this stage taste and add more of each if required. Season with salt and pepper to taste and serve straight away or freeze for future use.

Bread & Muffins

I am a huge fan of making my own muffins as they are super easy
to make and they freeze really well. I can also pack in some fruit
and vegetables for extra nutrition. I have also included some
delicious banana, lemon and blueberry breads which my girls are
obsessed with making. There are plenty of recipes here that are
easy to make but are bound to impress family and friends.

Cheese Scones

A delicious twist on a regular scone, your child will adore the cheesy taste of these. Avocado, tomato, salsa - there are so many tasty toppings that can be added or just simply serve with butter.

Makes: 10 Scones

150g self raising flour, extra for dusting
70g wholemeal flour
1 tsp baking powder
90g Cheddar cheese, grated
2 tbsp olive oil
1 large egg, beaten
90ml full fat milk, plus extra for brushing

1. Preheat the oven to 200°C and dust a baking tray with flour.

2. Meanwhile, sift both flours and baking powder into a bowl, adding in any left in the sieve. Stir in the cheese and make a well in the centre.

3. Pour in the oil, egg and some of the milk. Mix together adding in more milk to get the right consistency.

4. Transfer the dough to a lightly floured work surface and knead briefly until smooth.

5. Roll out the dough to about 2 cm thick. Cut out the scones with a medium cutter and place on the oven tray. Glaze the tops with the extra milk and sprinkle a little cheese on top of each scone before putting in the oven.

6. Bake in the oven for 10-15 minutes or until golden brown and cooked through.

7. Allow to cool and serve with your choice of filling.

Pesto & Feta Puff Wheels

There are so many variations that can be made with this recipe. Make sure to always have some puff pastry in your freezer so they can be whipped up at any time to use up leftover pesto or to make a healthy addition to the lunchbox. Ham and cheese is another delicious combination or if you fancy something sweet try my chocolate spread (page 170). Let your child come up with their own fillings so that they are more likely to give them a try.

Makes: 12 Puff Wheels

320g pack of puff pastry sheets, thawed
45g pesto sauce (pg 158)
50g feta, crumbled
40g mozzarella, chopped

1. Preheat the oven to 190°C and line a baking tray with parchment paper.

2. On a lightly floured surface, roll out the pastry sheets.

3. Spread the pesto evenly over the sheets, leaving a border around the edges. Sprinkle over the cheeses.

4. Roll the pastry up like a log, rolling it away from you. Start small then roll tightly, keeping the filling inside.

5. Slice the log into pinwheels, about 2.5cm thick and place them on the baking tray. Leave a gap between each as they will puff up during the cooking.

6. Bake for 20 minutes until crispy and golden. Allow to cool before serving.

Vegetable Egg Muffins

Every parent wants to ensure their little one is getting their five a day, so snacks like these Vegetable Egg Muffins are great for getting a portion in. Children love muffins, so the familiar form will mean they will be excited to give these a try.

Makes: 12 Muffins

3 carrots, peeled and grated
1 yellow pepper, chopped
90g peas, frozen
90g tin sweetcorn, drained
8 large eggs
Salt and pepper
100g Cheddar cheese, grated

Tip: Broccoli and tomatoes also work well in vegetable muffins.

1. Preheat the oven to 190°C. Grease a muffin tin or use a silicone muffin tray.

2. In a large bowl, add the grated carrots, peppers, peas and sweetcorn and mix together.

3. Pour the mixture into the muffin cases, until each case is about ⅔ of the way full.

4. Prepare your egg mixture by cracking the eggs into a jug and lightly whisking. Season with salt and pepper.

5. Pour the egg mixture into the vegetable mix until each muffin case is about ¾ full.

6. Top each with some cheese and bake in the oven for about 20 minutes or until the muffins are set.

7. Allow to cool, and serve with some of my tomato salsa (page 163) or freeze for future use.

Apple & Blueberry Oat Muffins

The morning can be the most stressful time in a busy household and some children just aren't hungry first thing. While it's important that you encourage your child to eat a healthy breakfast sometimes this just doesn't happen. Having a healthy muffin on hand is the best option for your child to eat on their way to school.

Makes: 12 Muffins

100g plain flour
100g wholemeal flour
50g porridge oats
3 tsp baking powder
1 tsp ground cinnamon
50g caster sugar
2 medium apples, peeled and grated
1 egg
125ml natural yoghurt
125ml full fat milk
2 tbsp sunflower oil
75g blueberries

1. Preheat your oven to 190°C. Grease your muffin tin or use a silicone muffin tray.

2. In a bowl, mix together the flours, oats, baking powder, cinnamon and sugar.

3. Stir in the grated apple, making sure it is evenly distributed.

4. Whisk the egg together with the yoghurt, milk and oil in a separate bowl. Add to the dry mixture, and then add your blueberries. At this stage, it is important to mix gently until everything is well combined.

5. Spoon the mixture into the muffin tin then bake for 25-30 minutes until risen and golden brown.

6. Transfer to a wire rack to cool. Muffins can be frozen and will last for up to 3 months in your freezer.

Apple & Banana Muffins

These muffins are a firm favourite in my household and I have been making them since the girls were babies. They are refined sugar free, naturally sweet and made with nutritious fruit. The girls adore them, and they are just the thing to pack in your child's lunchbox as a healthy snack.

Makes: 12 Muffins

2 red apples, peeled and grated
150g butter
2 bananas
180g wholemeal flour
4 tsp baking powder
2 eggs, whisked

Tip: Make extra and freeze in a resealable food storage bag for future use.

1. Preheat the oven to 180°C. Grease a muffin tin or use a silicone muffin tray.

2. Put the grated apple and butter in a saucepan and cook on a medium to low heat for 5 minutes until soft. Peel and mash the banana.

3. Add the apple mixture and mashed bananas to a bowl and mix in the flour, baking powder and eggs.

4. Spoon the mixture into the muffin tin and bake for 20 minutes, or until well risen and firm to the touch.

5. Allow to cool in the tin for a few minutes. Transfer to a wire rack and cool completely before serving.

Ham & Cheese Muffins

These muffins are not only delicious but also a great way of getting a portion of protein and carbohydrate all in one. Perfect for little hands and a great addition to your child's lunchbox. Make sure to batch cook in advance so you have healthy meals on hand for busier days.

Makes: 12 Muffins

165g plain flour
110g wholemeal flour
1 tbsp baking powder
1 tsp caster sugar
125g cooked ham, chopped
125g Cheddar cheese, grated
2 tbsp chives
2 eggs
200ml buttermilk
90ml sunflower oil

Tip: Muffins are a great option for children who are not huge fans of sandwiches.

1. Preheat the oven to 200°C. Grease a muffin tin or use a silicone muffin tray.

2. Combine the flours, baking powder, sugar, ham, cheese and chives.

3. In a separate bowl mix the eggs, buttermilk and oil.

4. Make a well in the dry ingredients then pour in the wet and combine.

5. Divide the mixture into the muffin tin. Place in the oven for 20-30 minutes, until a knife inserted in the centre of a muffin comes out clean.

Dough Balls

Most children love dough balls when eating out and this is an easy recipe to make your own. Whenever I pack the girls' lunchbox with dough balls and some tomato sauce (page 154) they complain that every other child in the class wanted some! My recipe makes more than enough to batch cook and freeze for when they are required. To keep the dough balls warm for lunch they can be placed in a preheated food flask.

Makes: 25 Dough Balls

325g strong white flour, plus extra for dusting
250ml lukewarm water
1 x 7g sachet fast action yeast
2 tbsp olive oil, plus extra for greasing
⅓ tsp salt

1. Place the flour in a large bowl. Make a well in the middle and add the water, yeast, oil and salt. Mix with your hands to form a smooth dough.

2. Dust a clean work surface and your hands with flour. Knead the dough until it doesn't stick to your fingers but also isn't too dry. Add more flour or water if required.

3. Make the dough into a flat round shape and place in a large bowl covered for about 1 hour until it doubles in size.

4. Once the dough has doubled in size, knead again and divide into about 25 even sized balls.

5. Prepare your baking tray by greasing it with olive oil and dust with flour. Place the dough balls evenly across, so they are just touching. Cover with a damp tea towel and prove in a warm place for 30-45 minutes.

6. Meanwhile, preheat the oven to 200°C.

7. Bake for 15 -18 minutes or until golden brown. Serve straight away or allow to cool and freeze for future use.

BREAD & MUFFINS

Soda Bread

Whenever I bake this bread it definitely reminds me of my childhood. My mother always baked our breads and this was a favourite. No need for proving, this is a really quick and simple bread to prepare and have on hand for the school lunches.

Makes: 1 Loaf

450g strong white flour, plus extra for dusting
1 tsp of bicarbonate of soda
1 tsp sugar
A pinch of salt
350ml buttermilk
1 egg

Tip: Before freezing slice it up so you can remove as needed.

1. Preheat the oven to 200°C. Grease and dust your loaf tin with flour.

2. In a large bowl combine the flour, bicarbonate of soda, sugar and salt.

3. In a separate bowl add your buttermilk, then whisk in the egg.

4. Make a well in the centre of the dry ingredients, and then pour in the wet mixture. Add a little extra flour if you find the dough is too wet and sticky.

5. Turn onto a lightly floured board and gently knead, just enough to bring the dough together.

6. Place in your prepared loaf tin.

7. Bake for about 40 minutes until golden brown and tapping underneath produces a hollow sound. Serve with some butter and your child's favourite filling.

Focaccia

When I have time at the weekend I make a batch of this delicious focaccia bread and the girls love it in their lunchbox together with some warm soup. It's also perfect to use for sandwiches with your child's favourite fillings.

Makes: 1 Loaf

1kg strong white flour, plus extra for dusting
625ml lukewarm water
3 x 7g sachets fast action yeast
2 tbsp sugar
1 tbsp sea salt (plus extra to top)
Olive oil

Tip: Check out page 131 for my Chicken and Avocado Focaccia Sandwich.

1. Place the flour in a large bowl. Make a well in the middle and add the water, yeast, sugar and salt. Mix with your hands to form a smooth dough.

2. Dust a clean work surface and your hands with flour, then knead the dough until it doesn't stick to your fingers but also isn't too dry. Add more flour or water as needed.

3. Make the dough into a flat round shape and place in a large bowl covered for about 1 hour. It should double in size.

4. To make your focaccia, knead the dough again and roll out to fit your baking tin.

5. Prepare your baking tray by greasing it with olive oil and dusting the flour. Place the dough on top and press your fingers into the dough to make indentations.

6. Sprinkle on some salt and drizzle with more olive oil. Cover with a tea towel and place somewhere warm for an hour.

7. Preheat your oven to 200°C.

8. Bake for 20 to 25 minutes, or until golden brown.

9. Cut into chunks and serve straight away or store in your fridge or freeze for future use.

BREAD & MUFFINS

Banana Bread

A huge hit in our house, this recipe is so easy to whip up when we have guests or when we just feel like baking. You can play around with it by adding chopped walnuts or chocolate chips.

Makes: 1 Loaf

Olive oil
125g butter, softened
120g caster sugar
3 large bananas
2 eggs
1 tsp of vanilla extract
250g self raising flour (plus extra for dusting)
1 tsp baking powder

Tip: Ripe bananas work best in this recipe. Bananas should have yellow skins (no green!) with an even smattering of brown freckles.

1. Preheat the oven to 180°C.

2. Lightly grease the bottom and sides of a 1 litre loaf tin with olive oil. Dust the sides of the tin lightly with flour, then tap to get rid of any excess.

3. In a large bowl beat the sugar and butter together using a wooden spoon until combined and smooth.

4. Peel the bananas and mash with the back of a fork and add them to the bowl along with the eggs and vanilla extract. Beat again for 1 minute.

5. Add in the flour and baking powder and mix well.

6. Pour the mixture into the loaf tin and bake for around 50 minutes, or until golden and cooked through.

7. To check if it's done, stick a skewer into the middle of the loaf, remove it after 5 seconds and if it comes out clean the loaf is cooked; if it's slightly sticky it needs a bit longer.

8. Allow the loaf to cool slightly, then carefully turn out on to a wire rack to cool completely.

9. Keep for up to 5 days in an airtight container or freeze for future use.

Blueberry Bread

Along with my Banana Bread this is one of my favourite treats. The yoghurt makes it lovely and moist and it freezes really well. If your child likes to help out with the cooking then give this recipe a go. It's so easy and they will love it!

Makes: 1 Loaf

Olive oil
150g blueberries, fresh or frozen
200g plain flour (plus extra
for dusting)
2 tsp baking powder
½ tsp salt
150g caster sugar
120g butter, softened
230g natural yoghurt
3 large eggs
2 tsp lemon zest
1 tsp vanilla extract

Tip: Swap out 100g of the plain flour for wholemeal flour to make it more nutritious.

1. Preheat the oven to 180°C. Lightly grease the bottom and sides of a 1 litre loaf tin with olive oil. Dust the sides of the tin lightly with flour, then tap to get rid of any excess.

2. Toss the blueberries in 1 tablespoon of the flour - this helps prevent them from sinking to the bottom when baking. In a medium bowl mix together the remaining flour, baking powder and salt.

3. In a large bowl beat the sugar and butter together using a wooden spoon until smooth. Add in the yoghurt, eggs, lemon zest and vanilla, and blend until well combined.

4. Combine the wet and dry ingredients making sure there are no lumps. Mix in the blueberries.

5. Pour the mixture into the loaf tin, then bake for around 50 minutes, or until golden and cooked through.

6. To check if it's done, stick a skewer into the middle of the loaf, remove it after 5 seconds and if it comes out clean the loaf is cooked; if it's slightly sticky it needs a bit longer.

7. Allow the loaf to cool slightly, then carefully turn out on to a wire rack to cool completely.

Lemon Bread

Full of flavour, this moist, dense, and rich recipe is one everyone will enjoy.

Makes: 1 Loaf

Olive oil
110g butter, softened
150g sugar
2 large eggs
120ml full fat milk
180g plain flour (plus extra
for dusting)
1 tsp baking powder
½ tsp salt
1½ tsp lemon zest

1. Preheat the oven to 180°C.

2. Lightly grease the bottom and sides of a 1 litre loaf tin with olive oil. Dust the sides of the tin lightly with flour, then tap to get rid of any excess.

3. In a large bowl beat the sugar and butter together using a wooden spoon until combined and smooth.

4. Add the eggs and milk and blend until well combined.

5. In a second bowl mix the flour, baking powder, salt and lemon zest.

6. Combine the wet ingredients with the dry ingredients to create your batter.

7. Pour the mixture into the loaf tin, then bake for around 50 minutes, or until golden and cooked through.

8. To check if it's done, stick a skewer into the middle of the loaf, remove it after 5 seconds and if it comes out clean the loaf is cooked; if it's slightly sticky it needs a bit longer.

9. Allow the loaf to cool slightly, then carefully turn out on to a wire rack to cool completely.

10. Keep for up to 5 days in an airtight container or freeze for future use.

Salads

Not often a section you see in a child-friendly recipe book.
I have included recipes with foods that your child is already
familiar with, simply put together as salads. From Fruity
Couscous to Tomato and Chickpea Pasta Salad there is plenty
here for every type of eater from the adventurous to the picky,
adapt as you see fit.

Roasted Red Pepper & Sweetcorn Pasta Salad

Pasta salad is a great option for a school lunch and can easily be put together with your child's favourite cheeses and vegetables. Cook a little extra pasta for dinner the night before to make it really easy to put together a delicious lunch the next day.

Makes: 4 Adult Portions

300g dried pasta of your choice
2 tbsp olive oil
3 red peppers, halved with seeds removed
225g sweetcorn
100g mozzarella cheese, chopped

Tip: The trick to getting children eating salads is to start by giving them vegetables that they already like then gradually introduce new vegetables.

1. Bring a large saucepan of water to the boil, add your pasta and a pinch of salt. Cook according to the packet instructions.

2. Once the pasta is ready strain and drizzle with olive oil. Set aside to cool.

3. Preheat your grill to its highest setting. Place the peppers on a wire rack skin side up and grill until the skins have gone black and look charred.

4. Transfer the peppers to a resealable food storage bag. Close tightly and leave to cool for about 10-15 minutes.

5. Remove the peppers from the bag and peel the skins. Slice the peppers into small manageable pieces.

6. In a large bowl combine the pasta, peppers, sweetcorn and cheese.

7. Serve straight away or place in your refrigerator to add to a lunchbox the next day. Pasta salad will keep in your fridge for up to 3 days.

Cucumber, Tomato & Basil Pasta Salad

Fresh and easy, this pasta salad is especially delicious in the summer months when tomatoes are nice and ripe. If your child is a fan of cucumber sticks and tomatoes they will love this recipe.

Makes: 4 Adult Portions

300g dried pasta of your choice
3 tbsp olive oil
2 cloves of garlic, minced
1 tbsp red wine vinegar
2 large tomatoes, finely chopped
¼ cucumber, finely chopped
Handful of fresh basil, roughly chopped

1. Bring a saucepan of water to the boil, add your pasta and a pinch of salt. Cook according to the packet instructions.

2. In a small saucepan over a low heat, add the oil, garlic and vinegar and cook for 2-3 minutes until infused.

3. Once the pasta has finished cooking, strain off the water and mix in the oil mix while still warm.

4. Stir in the tomatoes, cucumber and basil. Serve straight away or allow to cool and place in your refrigerator.

Tomato & Chickpea Pasta Salad

This recipe is fresh and simple and comes together fast. Chickpeas are high in protein and fibre which makes this an incredibly nutritious lunch option. If your child loves the crunch of a chickpea they should enjoy giving this a try. You can easily switch out anything they don't like, like tomatoes for sweetcorn or peppers. This salad can be served warm or cold in your child's food flask.

Makes: 4 x Portions

225g wholemeal pasta
65g cherry tomatoes, cut in half
200g tin chickpeas, rinsed and drained
170g Cheddar cheese, cubed
1 tbsp extra virgin olive oil
Salt and pepper

Tip: To get your child loving chickpeas try out my Roasted Savoury and Sweet Chickpeas on page 194-195.

1. Bring a saucepan of water to the boil, add your pasta and a pinch of salt. Cook pasta according to the packet instructions.

2. Toss the warm pasta with the tomatoes, chickpeas, cheese and olive oil and season to taste.

3. Serve warm straight away or refrigerate for future use.

Coleslaw

This is a lovely fresh take on a traditional coleslaw. I like having coleslaw in the fridge to make up a quick sandwich or serve as part of a BBQ. If your child isn't too sure about the vibrant red cabbage you can just use white cabbage. Gradually add in red cabbage until your child is accepting.

Makes: 4 Adult portions

¼ white cabbage, finely shredded
¼ red cabbage, finely shredded
2 carrots, peeled into ribbons
2 Granny Smith apples, grated

For the dressing:
1 tbsp extra virgin olive oil
1 lemon, juiced
freshly ground black pepper
1 tbsp pumpkin seeds
1 tbsp Greek yoghurt

1. Shred your ingredients by using your food processor. If you do not have a food processor then chop the cabbage by hand and grate the carrot and apple on a cheese grater.

2. Combine all the vegetables in a bowl and add your olive oil and lemon juice. Stir well so that all the ingredients mix together.

3. Add in your black pepper, seeds and yoghurt, stirring well and tasting until you have the flavour you like.

4. Serve straight away or store in your fridge for up to 3 days.

Potato Salad

If your child is a fan of potato salad when enjoying a BBQ, then why not offer it as a lunchbox filler. This recipe is super easy to put together - just make sure you save some potatoes from the night before and it will only take two minutes to assemble in the morning.

Makes: 4 Adult portions

500g potatoes, scrubbed and halved
1 tbsp crème fraiche
1 tbsp mayonnaise
2 spring onions, chopped finely
1 tsp mustard
Salt and pepper

Tip: You can bake potatoes overnight in a slow cooker by wrapping each potato in foil, and cooking on low for 7 to 8 hours.

1. Place the potatoes in a saucepan of lightly salted boiling water. Cover and simmer for 15 minutes or until tender then drain and allow to cool.

2. In a bowl mix together the remaining ingredients and carefully stir in the potatoes. Season to taste.

Fruity Couscous

A fresh and tasty couscous salad recipe that your child will love. Mix in extra vegetables and nuts of your choice for an added health kick.

Makes: 4 Adult portions

4 tbsp olive oil
1 tsp ground cumin
1 tsp ground coriander
½ tsp mild chili powder
35g sultanas
250g couscous
1 yellow pepper, finely chopped

Tip: Thinly sliced celery is great for an extra bit of crunch.

1. Heat the olive oil in a small frying pan over a low heat. Add in the spices and cook gently for a few minutes.

2. When the oil begins to infuse, remove from the heat. Add the sultanas and leave to stand for a few minutes, until they have softened.

3. Cook the couscous according to it's packet instructions.

4. In a bowl, mix the couscous, peppers, oil mixture and sultanas until well combined.

5. Serve straight away or allow to cool and refrigerate.

Sandwiches & Wraps

Sandwiches don't have to be plain and boring. In this section I have given you plenty of alternatives such as sandwich kebabs for a child who doesn't like it all mushed together, to roll-ups and pinwheels! Every sandwich and wrap is built on the principle that each meal should include a carbohydrate, protein, fruit and/or vegetable. Remember this when putting yours together or allowing your child to choose their favourite fillings.

Sandwich Kebabs

Forget about boring cheese sandwiches; a kebab allows you to be much more experimental. Lots of children don't like particular sandwiches for many reasons. Whether it's because tomatoes make their bread too moist or they don't like cheese paired with turkey, sandwich kebabs are the perfect solution. By placing the ingredients on a stick and serving them with a dip separately they stay much fresher. Get your child involved in making them up and they will definitely become a big hit in your house.

Makes: 4 Skewers

1 ciabatta or ¼ stick of French bread, cubed
80g mozzarella and/or Cheddar cheese cubed
50g chorizo, sliced
1 yellow pepper, sliced
4 cherry tomatoes
4 skewers

1. Thread a skewer with bread, cheese, chorizo and vegetables in any order.

2. Repeat with the remaining skewers and ingredients.

3. Serve with homemade pesto (page 157) for dipping.

Tip: If you don't have any skewers to hand simply place each element in different portion pots.

Smoked Salmon & Cream Cheese Pinwheels

Rolling up sandwiches like a pinwheel makes sandwiches more fun. Pinwheels are also the perfect size for little fingers.

Makes: 12 to 14 Pinwheels

3 slices of wholemeal bread
40g cream cheese
120g smoked salmon, sliced

1. Use a rolling pin to roll the bread out, flat and thin. Remove the crust if you wish.

2. On each slice, spread on a layer of cream cheese then a thin layer of smoked salmon.

3. Tightly roll up the slices of bread and squeeze the rolls together gently to secure. Use a serrated knife to cut the rolls into 4 or 5 pieces.

Veggie Tortilla Roll-Ups

I am always looking for new ways to get vegetables into my girls' sandwiches. They both like different vegetables so I often change this recipe up to suit both their tastes. A good tip is to not overfill the tortillas so you can easily shape them into pinwheels.

Makes: 2 Portions

60g cream cheese
35g Cheddar cheese, grated
60g sour cream
½ yellow pepper, finely chopped
1 carrot, grated
1 tbsp parsley, finely chopped (optional)
2 wholemeal or plain flour tortillas

1. In a bowl mix the cheeses, sour cream, vegetables and parsley until combined.

2. Spread half of the mixture on one side of a tortilla and tightly roll it. Repeat with the second tortilla.

3. If time allows, wrap in cling film and refrigerate for 3 hours.

4. To serve, cut the tortilla roll into 2cm slices.

Tip: To avoid any of the filling from spilling out during the wrapping process, make sure vegetables are evenly spread and only on half of the tortilla.

Chicken Quesadillas

Quesadillas are one of my favourite meals. I started making these for my girls as a finger food when they were babies. Over the years we have got more and more adventurous with the fillings. For a vegetarian option use chopped red peppers.

Makes: 2 Portions

20g Cheddar cheese, grated
1 spring onion, finely chopped
60g chicken, cooked and cubed
2 flour tortillas

Accompaniments
Sour cream or Greek yoghurt
Tomato salsa (pg 163)

Tip: Make sure not to overfill your tortilla or the filling will fall out.

1. In a bowl mix the cheese, onion and chicken. Spread the mixture evenly on a tortilla then layer the second tortilla on top.

2. If you are preparing the night before refrigerate overnight.

3. To serve, heat a non-stick frying pan over a medium heat. Cook each side for a minute and a half until you have a crispy outside and the cheese is melted. Cut into wedges and serve.

4. To keep warm you can wrap the wedges in tinfoil and place in your food flask.

Mozzarella Pesto Melt

Pesto and cheese is a fab combination! This is equally divine without heating it on a pan - just use ciabatta bread instead for a delicious sandwich.

Makes: 1 Portion

2 slices wholemeal bread
Butter
60g mozzarella, chopped
1 tbsp Nut-Free Pesto (pg 159)

Tip: In order to keep your mozzarella fresh once opened, store in your portion pot with cold water. Change the water every other day.

1. Spread butter on your sliced bread.

2. Lay one slice of bread, butter side down, on a preheated pan over a medium heat.

3. Layer the mozzarella and pesto on the bread.

4. Top with the second slice of bread - butter side up.

5. Cook for about a minute until nice and golden and then flip and cook on the other side.

6. Serve straight away or cut up into smaller bites and wrap in tinfoil and place in a preheated flask.

Tuna & Sweetcorn Sandwich

This is a regular in my girls' lunchbox. I love that I can whip this up at any time without having much food in the fridge. Simply make sure you always have a tin of sweetcorn and tuna in your cupboard and you are sorted. I usually opt for a low salt version of tinned sweetcorn or alternatively you can use frozen sweetcorn which you will need to defrost first.

Makes: 2 Portions

4 tbsp sweetcorn, drained
2 tbsp mayonnaise
1 tin tuna, drained
4 slices of wholemeal bread

1. Mix the sweetcorn, mayonnaise and tuna together in a bowl.

2. Spread the mixture on your bread and remove crusts if you wish.

3. Cut each sandwich into 4 bite size pieces.

Omelette Wrap

It can be difficult to come up with different bread options each week. This recipe replaces a tortilla with an egg omelette for added nutrition. It has a really nice texture and you can serve it with your child's favourite filling.

Makes: 1 Wrap

1 tsp olive oil
2 eggs, lightly beaten
1 spring onion, finely sliced
¼ red pepper, deseeded and cut into strips
1 tsp fresh ginger, grated
1 tsp toasted sesame seeds
1 tsp sesame oil
1 tsp soy sauce

Tip: Serve with some toasted wholemeal fingers.

1. Heat the oil in a frying pan over a medium heat. Pour in the egg, swirl and tilt the pan until it covers the base. When the egg starts to set, bring the edges to the centre and allow the uncooked egg to run into the spaces. Flip over and cook for a few seconds on the other side. When cooked remove from the pan and allow to cool.

2. In a bowl add your vegetables, ginger, sesame seeds, oil and soy sauce and mix to combine.

3. Spoon the mixture into the centre of the omelette then roll it up.

4. Serve straight away or to serve warm for school, cut into quarters wrap in tinfoil and add to your preheated food flask.

Smashed Chickpea & Roasted Pepper Sandwich

I love to have some of my Smashed Chickpea Spread (page 169) in the fridge to whip up a quick nutritious sandwich. For this recipe you can prepare the red pepper by either grilling or roasting it in the oven. Alternatively when time is tight you can buy roasted red peppers in a jar - just make sure it is low in salt.

Makes: 1 portion

2 slices of wholemeal bread
Butter
1 tbsp Smashed Chickpea Spread (pg 169)
15g roasted red pepper, skinned and diced
Handful of lettuce leaves

Tip: If this is new to your child then my advice is to offer a deconstructed sandwich so that they can add on the spread and lettuce at school. This will encourage them to give it a try!

1. Butter your sandwich and then spread on the chickpea mixture. Fill with some roasted red pepper and lettuce leaves.

2. Cut into your child's favourite sandwich size pieces.

Chicken & Avocado Focaccia

This is a great way of using up leftover roast chicken from a dinner. You can also add in your child's favourite salad vegetables like tomatoes and peppers.

Makes: 1 Sandwich

½ avocado, chopped
1 tsp lemon juice
1 tsp mayonnaise
Salt & pepper to taste
1 slice focaccia bread (pg 98)
Slices of cooked chicken

Tip: If you do not have any focaccia bread, ciabatta bread works equally well.

1. In a bowl mix the avocado, lemon juice and mayonnaise. Add salt and pepper to taste.

2. Cut the focaccia bread in half and spread the avocado mixture on one side.

3. Layer with some sliced chicken, then top with the other focaccia slice.

4. Cut into manageable pieces and add to your child's lunchbox.

Mediterranean Pita Pocket

If your child is a fan of olives they will adore this combination. For added freshness you can leave the mixture in a portion pot and get your child to fill up their own pita pocket at school.

Makes: 2 Portions

½ cucumber, cubed
1 tomato, cubed
6 black olives, chopped
30g feta cheese, crumbled
4 basil leaves, finely chopped
1 tbsp hummus (page 167)
2 pita pockets, sliced in half

Tip: For a warm crispy version pop the pita pocket into the toaster before adding in your filling.

1. In a bowl, combine the cucumber, tomato, olives, feta and basil.

2. Spread some hummus on the inside of the pitas then fill them with your mixture.

Pasta & Sauces

When making up my girls' lunch I use a food flask
for about three out of five school days. They love a warm
lunch and especially pasta. To change it up and to have
healthy nut-free sauces on hand I always batch cook at
the weekend. I only have to make one sauce each
week and it lasts for a month. These recipes are
also perfect for mid-week meals.

Quick Bolognese

Who doesn't love Bolognese? I have created this quick and easy version to provide parents with a healthy lunchbox idea that they can turn to again and again. As so many children adore Bolognese, this is a wonderful dish to use to encourage them to eat all of their lunch. A favourite dinner will be a welcome sight in a picky eater's food flask, as it will make them feel comfortable. Of course, this is not just a recipe for children! This is also a fantastic recipe to batch cook or whip up when you are pushed for time.

Makes: 4 Adult Portions

1 tbsp olive oil
1 onion
1 large carrot
1 celery stalk
1 garlic clove, minced
450g quality minced beef
250ml passata
100ml low salt beef stock
Pinch of dried thyme

Tip: Remove from the freezer the night before so you can reheat and add to fresh pasta.

1. Use a blender or processor to finely chop the onion, carrots and celery so that they will cook quicker. Make sure to use the pulse button rather then blend.

2. Heat the olive oil in a large saucepan over a medium heat and then cook the onion, celery and carrot for about 5 minutes until they have softened. Add the garlic and cook for a further 1 minute.

3. Stir in the meat and sauté for 5 minutes before adding in the passata, stock and dried thyme.

4. Cover and cook over a low to medium heat for about 12 minutes.

5. Serve with your choice of pasta.

Chicken & Broccoli Bake

Deliciously cheesy, this bake has been a family favourite for a long time now. This is one of my mid-week 20 minute meals and I always make extra so that we can have leftovers in our food flasks. It also freezes really well.

Makes: 4 Adult Portions

1 tbsp olive oil
4 skinless chicken breasts, cubed
350g of dried macaroni
1 head of broccoli, separated into florets
3 tbsp butter
3 tbsp flour
100ml full fat milk
300g Cheddar cheese, grated
50g breadcrumbs

1. Heat the oil in a large frying pan over a medium heat. Add the chicken pieces and fry until golden and cooked through. Set aside.

2. Boil the broccoli florets with the macaroni. Cook the pasta according to the packet instructions (usually about 6-8 minutes).

3. Strain and allow to cool slightly while you prepare the cheese sauce.

4. In a small saucepan melt the butter. Stir in the flour until it forms a paste. Gradually whisk in the milk, until smooth with no lumps.

5. Bring the mixture to the boil. Remove from the heat and stir in 200g of the cheese.

6. Stir the sauce into the macaroni and broccoli mix.

7. Meanwhile, preheat your grill.

8. Place the chicken, macaroni and broccoli mix into a large oven proof dish. Scatter the bread crumbs and remaining cheese over the top. Place under the grill for 3-4 minutes until golden and crispy.

Slow Cooker Butternut Squash Lasagne

This slow cooker lasagne is so delicious my girls never miss the meat - though they don't let me call it lasagne! I love my slow cooker and it's great for a busy family. This recipe takes more time because you need to layer it but it's definitely worth the effort.

Makes: 6 Adult Portions

500g ricotta
1 egg
Salt and pepper
½ tsp nutmeg
1 small bunch of kale or spinach, chopped
2 x 400g tins chopped tomatoes
9 oven ready lasagne sheets
1 butternut squash, peeled and cut into 1cm slices
190g Gouda or Jack cheese, grated
35g Parmesan cheese, grated

Tip: Use oven ready lasagne sheets, otherwise you will need to blanch them before cooking.

1. In a bowl, mix the ricotta, egg, salt, pepper and nutmeg.

2. Gently fold in the spinach or kale. Set aside.

3. In a slow cooker, spread ½ a tin of tomatoes along the base. Top with 3 lasagne sheets, breaking as needed to fit. Spread ⅓ of the ricotta mixture on top. Next layer butternut squash slices, overlapping if necessary to fit. Spread ½ a tin of tomatoes and top with half the grated Gouda or Jack cheese.

4. Repeat step 3, starting and ending with lasagne sheets.

5. Add another ½ a can of tomatoes. Top with remaining ricotta mixture and Gouda or Jack cheese.

6. Cover and cook on low for 4 hours.

7. Remove the lid and sprinkle with Parmesan cheese. Replace lid and turn off slow cooker. Leave to sit for 15 minutes before serving.

One Pot Lasagne

As a busy mum, I like cooking meals that are fast and simple. Traditional lasagne can be time consuming to prepare, but not this one! It's an easier version of the classic Italian favourite and is cooked in one pot - meaning less dishes to wash.

Makes: 4 Adult Portions

1 portion of my Quick Bolognese sauce (pg 137)
250g oven ready lasagne sheets
500g crème fraiche
50g Parmesan cheese, grated
1 ball of mozzarella, thinly sliced
Handful fresh basil leaves, roughly torn

Tip: Because you may be using pre-cooked Bolognese use up straight away as this cannot be reheated.

1. In a large pot, place a layer of bolognese followed by the lasagne sheets - breaking as needed to fit, creme fraiche, Parmesan cheese and the sheets again.

2. Continue assembling until the last layer is done. Top with mozzarella and basil leaves.

3. Cover the pan with a lid and let it cook gently over a low heat for 20 minutes.

4. Serve immediately or send to school in your child's warm food flask.

Roasted Vegetables Pasta Bake

This delicious pasta is tossed in homemade pesto sauce and roasted vegetables, topped with cheese and baked in the oven until the cheese is melted and piping hot. Yummy! Pesto is always a great hit in our house and this pasta bake recipe also allows for more vegetables to be added. I find that my girls are more likely to try new vegetables with their favourite sauce on top.

Makes: 6 Adult Portions

2 red onions, chopped
1 aubergine, chopped
2 courgettes, chopped
2 red peppers, chopped
2 yellow peppers, chopped
4 tbsp olive oil
500g fusilli pasta
4 tbsp pesto (pg 157)
250ml crème fraiche
Freshly ground black pepper
150g Cheddar cheese, grated

Tip: If adding to a food flask make sure you use my Nut-Free Pesto on page 159.

1. Preheat the oven to 200°C.

2. Place your chopped vegetables on a roasting tray and drizzle with olive oil.

3. Roast for about 25-30 minutes, until soft and slightly brown on the edges. Turn them over half way through cooking.

4. Meanwhile, bring a large saucepan of water to the boil. Add the pasta and cook for about 6 minutes. Since you will be cooking the pasta for a second time in the oven, you want to make sure the inside is still hard.

5. Add the pesto and crème fraiche into a saucepan, season with ground black pepper and heat gently.

6. Mix the pasta and vegetables into the sauce. Spoon the mixture into an ovenproof dish and sprinkle the cheese on top.

7. Cover the dish with tinfoil and bake in the oven for 25-30 minutes. Remove the tinfoil for the last 2-3 minutes.

8. Top with some extra cheese and serve.

Easy Peasy Tortelloni

This is the perfect recipe to make up in the morning before school. Just make sure you have your Alfredo sauce prepared and have some fresh Tortelloni to hand in the fridge. You can also use dried pasta but just remember it needs a longer cooking time.

Choose your child's favourite Tortelloni filling. There's so many options from ham and cheese to ricotta and spinach. Pop it into a heated flask and voila! A super delicious healthy lunch.

Makes: 2 Child Portions

125g fresh Tortelloni
30g frozen peas
90g alfredo sauce (pg 153)

Tip: Pop grated Parmesan cheese into a portion pot so your child can sprinkle it on at school.

1. Cook the Tortelloni according to the packet instructions. Add your peas 2-3 minutes towards the end of the cooking time.

2. Meanwhile heat your food flask and your alfredo sauce.

3. Drain your Tortelloni and peas and toss it in the heated alfredo sauce.

4. Pack in a preheated food flask and place into your child's lunch bag.

Cauliflower Macaroni & Cheese

This Mac and Cheese recipe appears weekly in our household. I like to cook the entire bag of macaroni so that I have enough leftover for the school lunch the next day. I have converted many a child with a cauliflower aversion to love this dish. It's light and cheesy and you can add extra vegetables, slices of cooked chicken or cooked prawns.

Makes: 5 Adult Portions

500g dried macaroni
1 small head of cauliflower, finely chopped
200g Cheddar cheese, grated
100g Parmesan cheese, grated
200ml crème fraiche
1 tsp dried parsley

TIp: For a more crunchy version, top with breadcrumbs and place under a grill for 10 minutes.

1. Add the macaroni and cauliflower to salted boiling water and cook according the macaroni packet instructions.

2. Mix the grated cheeses, crème fraiche and parsley in a heatproof glass or metal bowl.

3. On a hob, boil water in a small saucepan. Place the bowl with the cheese mixture over the boiling water and allow the cheese to melt. Keep the temperature low so that it does not boil over and keep stirring until the cheese has melted.

4. Drain the macaroni and cauliflower and reserve some of the cooking liquid.

5. In a large dish add the macaroni, cauliflower and cheese and mix through. At this stage you can add some of the cooking water to thin it out, if needed.

6. Place it in the centre of the table and allow your child to take their own portion. I promise you they will be back for seconds!

7. Store in the fridge for up to 3 days and heat through before placing it into your child's food flask.

Marinara Sauce

Pasta with Marinara sauce is a go-to dish for so many busy parents, including myself. This classic combination is quick, simple and children adore it! The leftovers even make for a stress-free school lunch the next day. I know it can be tempting during hectic weeks to reach for a shop bought jar, but I promise you that my tasty homemade Marinara recipe is easy and fast to make. It is filled to the brim with fresh veggies, which can be sneakily blended to a smooth consistency so fussy eaters won't notice. My girls love it, and I am sure your little ones will too!

Makes: 4 Adult Portions

2 tbsp olive oil
1 onion, finely chopped
100g cauliflower, roughly chopped
100g yellow pepper, roughly chopped
100g sweet potato, peeled and roughly chopped
100g butternut squash, peeled and roughly chopped
2 x 400g tin chopped tomatoes
Salt and pepper
Handful of basil, finely chopped

Tip: For a fussy eater after they have eaten and enjoyed this, let them know all the veggies in it and praise them for eating them.

1. Heat the olive oil in a large saucepan over a medium heat. Add the chopped vegetables and cook for 10 minutes with the lid on until the vegetables are soft.

2. Add in the tinned tomatoes and season with salt and pepper if using. Simmer on a medium to low heat for a further 20 minutes. Place the lid back on during this time but leave it ajar so that some heat escapes.

3. Stir in the basil and simmer for a further 3-4 minutes.

4. Place the sauce in a blender or food processor and blend to your desired consistency.

3. Serve straight away with pasta or store in your portion pots and freeze for future use.

Tomato & Mascarpone Sauce

A really delicious and simple pasta sauce that can be prepared in advance and then heated up before school to take in your child's food flask. Add cooked chicken and some greens for an evening meal.

Makes: 4 Adult portions

2 tbsp olive oil
1 onion, finely chopped
1 clove of garlic, finely chopped
1 tbsp parsley, chopped
1 tbsp basil, chopped
400g tin chopped tomatoes
Salt and pepper
85ml water
225g mascarpone cheese

1. Heat the olive oil in a frying pan over a medium heat.

2. Add the onion and garlic and cook until very soft, but not coloured.

3. Stir in the herbs and cook for 1 minute. Stir in the tomatoes and add seasoning to taste.

4. Add in the water, bring to the boil and allow the sauce to bubble gently for 30 minutes.

5. Stir in the mascarpone and mix until melted.

6. To serve, pour over pasta and store in your food flask for an easy school lunch.

Easy Carbonara

This is my go-to recipe when I have no sauce prepared for the girls' lunch. It also works well as a mid-week family meal that takes minutes to prepare. It is not a sauce that keeps very well so do make it up on the morning before school.

Makes: 2 Flask Portions

100g spaghetti or pasta of choice
Handful of frozen peas
2 eggs, beaten
20g Parmesan cheese, grated

Tip: Fill the flask to the top to make sure no heat escapes and your child will have delicious warm pasta come lunch time.

1. Cook your spaghetti according to the packet instructions.

2. Meanwhile bring a second saucepan of water to the boil, add your frozen peas and drain after 2-3 minutes.

3. Drain the spaghetti, reserving a little of the cooking water.

4. Return the pasta and peas to the saucepan and, working quickly, stir through the eggs and Parmesan. Keep stirring until there is no liquid left.

5. Fill a preheated food flask and include in your child's lunchbox.

Alfredo Sauce

I'm not a huge fan of cream in sauces but I do love Alfredo sauce. So for a healthier version I have made this with milk and cream cheese and the girls love it. It's so easy to prepare and I make sure I have a batch of it cooked in the freezer. Try it with my Easy Peasy Tortelloni recipe on page 144.

Makes: 4 Adult Portions

125g unsalted butter
3 cloves of garlic, minced
225g cream cheese
¼ tsp oregano
¼ tsp basil
240ml full fat milk
100g Parmesan cheese, grated
Freshly ground black pepper

1. Melt the butter in a large saucepan over a medium to low heat. Add the minced garlic and saute until softened for about 1 minute.

2. Add the cream cheese and the dried herbs. Keep stirring and start to add your milk, slowly, continuing to stir.

3. Add the Parmesan cheese and pepper. Stir well to combine.

has reached the desired thickness.

4. Serve straight away with some pasta and vegetables or store in your portion pots and freeze for future use.

Tomato Sauce

This is my go to tomato sauce recipe which I make up a batch of each week. I freeze small portions for a quick and easy flask lunch, then larger portions for when I use it with meatballs and for spreading on a pizza.

Makes: 4 Adult Portions

4 tbsp olive oil
4 cloves of garlic, minced
1 tbsp tomato purée
2 x 400g tins chopped tomatoes
Handful of basil, chopped

Tip: If you have more time, cook this sauce on a lower heat for longer. The longer you cook the tomatoes, the more flavour the sauce will develop.

1. Heat the olive oil in a large saucepan over a medium to low heat. Add in the garlic and cook for 3-4 minutes.

2. Stir in the tomato purée and cook for a further 2 minutes. Add in the chopped tomatoes.

3. Bring the mixture to the boil. Reduce the heat and simmer for 15-20 minutes, until the sauce has thickened.

4. Stir in the basil and simmer for a further 3-4 minutes.

5. Place the sauce in a blender or food processor and blend to your desired consistency.

6. Serve with your choice of pasta or portion and freeze for future use.

Spicy Tomato Sauce

You might be surprised by how much a child likes spicy foods. Right from the weaning stages I would advice adding a little spice to your child's meals. Increase or decrease the amount of chilli in this recipe based on your child's preference. This sauce is especially nice with meatballs so be sure to make some extra for the freezer.

Makes: 4 Adult Portions

1 tbsp olive oil
1 red chilli, deseeded and finely chopped
1 onion, finely chopped
3 cloves of garlic, minced
2 tbsp tomato purée
200ml low salt vegetable stock
400g tin chopped tomatoes
Salt and pepper

1. Heat the olive oil in a large saucepan over a medium to low heat. Add the chilli and onion and cook on a low heat for 8 minutes, until softened.

2. Add in the garlic and cook for 3-4 minutes.

3. Stir in the tomato purée, vegetable stock, chopped tomatoes and season with salt and pepper. Bring the mixture to the boil. Reduce the heat and simmer for 15-20 minutes, until the sauce has thickened.

4. Place the sauce in a blender or food processor and blend to your desired consistency.

5. Serve with your choice of pasta or portion and freeze for future use.

Pestos & Spreads

I simply just had to have a section on pestos!
Children love them and you can make so many different
varieties while also getting vegetables in, perfect for any
picky child. I also love spreads because this is what makes a
plain sandwich both nutritious and exciting. Give my salsa,
pestos and hummus recipes a go and you won't be stuck on
what to add to your child's sandwich.

Basil & Courgette Pesto

You will be pleasantly surprised at how creamy and delicious this pesto is. Your child may never even suspect it contains raw vegetables - win win! Bursting with fresh flavours, this recipe is a delicious twist on my Basil Pesto. Who knew adding courgettes would result in such a creamy, flavourful sauce? Swirl it into pasta for a quick and healthy lunchtime meal your children will love. Swap out the pine nuts for pumpkin seeds to make this nut-free.

Makes: 4 Adult Portions

40g pine nuts
½ courgette
2 handfuls of basil
1 clove of garlic
Squeeze of lemon juice
2 tbsp extra virgin olive oil
50g Parmesan, grated
Ground black pepper

Tip: Place pesto in an airtight portion pot. Add a layer of olive oil to preserve it for longer.

1. In a frying pan over a medium heat, lightly toast the pine nuts. Remove from the heat and allow to cool.

2. Roughly chop the courgette. Add the courgette, basil, garlic, pine nuts and lemon juice to a food processor. Pulse until a loose paste forms.

3. Add in the olive oil while the blender is running and pulse until everything is combined. Add more oil if needed to get the right texture.

4. Stir in your Parmesan and black pepper to taste.

Nut-Free Basil Pesto

As most schools now have a nut-free policy, I created this by using sunflower seeds instead of pine nuts. Fear not, this is equally as delicious as your traditional pesto.

Makes: 250g

50g sunflower seeds
Large bunch of basil leaves
½ clove of garlic
100ml extra virgin olive oil
Squeeze of lemon juice
35g Parmesan, grated
Ground black pepper

Tip: Pumpkin seeds also work well in this recipe.

1. Lightly toast the sunflower seeds on a dry pan and allow to cool.

2. Add the toasted seeds, basil, garlic, oil and lemon juice to a blender or food processor and blend until combined.

3. Stir in the grated Parmesan and black pepper to taste.

Broccoli Pesto

This is a great way of getting in your child's five-a-day and it's another nut-free recipe perfect for schools with a nut-free policy.

Makes: 4 Portions

350g broccoli (about one head), broken into florets
Handful of basil leaves
½ clove of garlic
100ml extra virgin olive oil
Squeeze of lemon juice
30g Parmesan, grated
Ground black pepper

Tip: Try this in my Mozzarella Pesto Melt on page 125.

1. Steam the broccoli for about 6 minutes until tender.

2. Add the broccoli, basil, garlic, olive oil and lemon juice to a blender and blend until combined.

3. Stir in the grated Parmesan and black pepper to taste.

Red Pepper Pesto

I love classic pesto but every once in a while I like to create different versions. Seeing as the girls like tomato sauce, red dips and of course pesto it wasn't hard to convince them to give this a try. I use it both as a spread on sandwiches and as a pasta sauce.

Makes: 4 Adult portions

4 red peppers, halved and deseeded
Handful of basil
50g pine nuts
2 cloves of garlic
1 tsp paprika
3 tbsp extra virgin olive oil
35g Parmesan cheese, grated
Ground black pepper

1. Preheat the grill to its highest setting. Place the peppers on a wire rack skin side up and grill until the skins have gone black and look charred.

2. Remove the peppers from the grill and place in a plastic food bag. Close it tightly and leave the peppers to cool for about 10-15 minutes.

3. Meanwhile, heat a large frying pan over a medium heat and lightly toast the pine nuts.

4. Remove the peppers from the bag and peel the skins.

5. Add the peppers, basil, pine nuts, garlic, paprika and olive oil to a blender and blend until combined.

6. Stir in your grated Parmesan and black pepper to taste.

Tomato Salsa & Crispy Tortilla

If you are looking for flavour, then look no further than this tasty Tomato Salsa! I always love to have some on hand as an accompaniment to fajitas night. For an exciting school lunch idea, pack this in your little one's lunchbox as a mild dip with your homemade crispy tortillas.

Makes: 450g

1 wholemeal tortilla
1 tsp extra virgin olive oil
4 tomatoes, roughly chopped
1 tbsp coriander, finely chopped
½ red onion, chopped
1 lime, juiced
Salt to taste

Tip: To keep your tortillas nice and fresh, allow to cool then place in your airtight portion pots.

1. Cut the tortilla in half and then into four wedges or six depending on the size. Heat the oil in a frying pan and fry the wedges in batches for about 2 minutes on each side until golden and crisp.

2. To make the salsa place all of the ingredients in a blender or food processor and blend to your desired consistency. Season to taste.

3. Pack in your child's lunchbox in a 90ml/3oz portion pot and serve with your toasted tortillas.

Avocado Hummus

This creamy hummus is a lovely alternative to the classic dish.

Makes: 400g

1 large ripe avocado,
400g tin chickpeas, drained
½ clove of garlic
4 tbsp tahini
Juice of 2 limes
¼ tsp cumin
4 tbsp extra virgin olive oil

Tip: To ripen the avocado place in a brown paper bag with an apple or a banana.

1. Add everything except the olive oil to a blender. Blend until smooth, for about 1 minute. With the motor running slowly add in the olive oil until light and creamy.

2. Store in an airtight portion pot for up to a week. Serve with my crispy tortillas on page 163.

Nut Butter

I like to make my own nut butters so that I know exactly what is going into them. If you are planning on using this as a spread for school lunches, seeds are also a great option. Anything from pumpkin seeds to sunflower seeds work great.

Makes: 150g

140g raw unsalted nuts
(such as almonds, peanuts,
cashews, macadamias etc.)
¼ tbsp of coconut oil

Tip: If you wish, you can add flavour to your nut butter by adding cinnamon, honey or maple syrup.

1. Blend the nuts in your food processor until they become coarsely ground. Scrape down the sides.

2. Add in the coconut oil and blend for a few more seconds until combined.

3. Store in an airtight container and place in your fridge. It will last for up to 2 weeks.

Pancakes & Waffles

Despite the heading you don't need a waffle maker for these recipes, simply prepare the waffles as pancakes. However if you can I would advise you invest in a waffle maker to give you lots of options. They are crispy and fluffy, their design makes them the perfect vehicle for toppings like syrup, and they can be sweet or savoury. Yummy!

Pancake Sandwiches

This recipes uses my fail-safe pancake mixture. If you usually make pancakes with white flour then a great way to get your children moving to wholemeal is to start with a half and half mixture. Pancake Sandwiches can easily be whipped up in the morning. I have suggested a few fillings but really anything goes so don't be afraid to experiment with sweet and savoury options.

Makes: 12 Small Pancakes

½ cup wholemeal flour
½ cup self raising flour
1 cup full fat milk
1 egg
Knob of unsalted butter

Suggested Fillings:
Grated cheese and salsa (pg 163)
Sliced meats like ham, chicken or salami
Sweetcorn and pesto (pg 157)
Chocolate spread (pg 170)
Cream cheese and nut butter (pg 173)
Grated apple and nut butter (pg 173)

Tip: Get yourself a cup measure to make this recipe even easier.

1. Whisk together the flour, milk and egg to make a smooth batter.

2. In a large frying pan, melt the butter over a medium heat.

3. Add the pancake mixture, one spoonful at a time. Cook until you see bubbles rising to the top. Flip over and cook on the other side for two minutes further.

4. At this stage if you are adding cheese, place the grated cheese on top of the pancake and allow to melt before removing from the pan.

5. Add your fillings then top the pancake with a second pancake and store in your child's lunchbox.

Sweetcorn Pancakes

These pancakes make a fantastic snack or lunchbox filler. Plan ahead and make the mixture the night before so it's quick and easy to prepare in the mornings before school. Pair with my homemade tomato sauce (page 154).

Makes: 10 Small Pancakes

120g self raising flour
240ml full fat milk
1 egg
85g tin sweetcorn, drained
2 spring onions, roughly chopped
30g feta cheese
Knob of unsalted butter

1. Whisk together the flour, milk and egg to make a smooth batter.

2. In a blender add your sweetcorn, spring onion and feta cheese, blend for about a minute. Add this mixture to your batter and whisk to combine.

3. In a large frying pan, melt the butter over a medium heat.

4. Add the pancake mixture, one spoonful at a time. Cook until you see bubbles rising to the top. Flip over and cook on the other side for two minutes further.

5. Serve warm or cool and refrigerate for up to 3 days.

Oaty Banana Pancakes

I had two reluctant banana eaters so over the years I have come up with different recipes to get them into their diets. This is an adaptation of my baby weaning banana pancakes. By adding in the oats it makes them more substantial and filling for a school going child.

Makes: 8 Small Pancakes

1 large banana
2 eggs, whisked
25g porridge oats
Pinch of baking powder
Dash of vanilla extract
Knob of unsalted butter

Tip: To keep the pancakes warm for school pop them into your preheated food flask.

1. Mash the banana and mix in the eggs, oats, baking powder and vanilla extract to form a batter.

2. In a large frying pan, melt the butter over a medium heat.

3. Add the pancake mixture, one spoonful at a time. Cook until you see bubbles rising to the top. Flip over and cook on the other side for two minutes further.

4. Remove from the heat and top with chopped fruit of your choice. Serve straight away or cool and refrigerate.

Apple Cinnamon Waffles

Who doesn't love apple and cinnamon - delish! These waffles are a real treat in our house. I love that I can make extra to freeze and simply pop them in a toaster when I want some. If your child isn't a fan of the apple chunks then purée the apple mixture and reduce the amount of milk to 400ml.

Makes: 2 Portions

60g butter
4 apples, peeled & chopped into small chunks
2 tsp cinnamon
120g self raising flour
120g wholemeal flour
2 tsp baking powder
500ml full fat milk
2 eggs
1 tsp vanilla extract

1. Place a pan over a medium heat and add the butter. Allow the butter to melt then add in the chopped apple and 1 tsp of cinnamon. Reduce the heat, and sauté until soft for about 3 minutes. Remove from the heat.

2. Preheat your waffle iron.

3. In a large bowl combine the flours, baking powder and the rest of the cinnamon.

4. In a separate bowl mix together the milk, eggs and vanilla extract.

5. Add the wet ingredient to the dry and stir, making sure not to overmix.

6. Stir in the sautéed apples and ensure the ingredients are well combined.

7. Pour a ladle of the mixture in the centre of the waffle maker and spread a little to the sides. Cook for 3 to 5 minutes or until golden brown.

8. Serve with your favourite toppings.

Potato & Carrot Waffles

One of my top tips on getting a fussy or picky eater to try new foods is to give them something they are familiar with. Most children love pancakes or waffles so why not add in some nutritious vegetables.

Makes: 6 Waffles

2 carrots, grated
1 large sweet potato, grated
125g Cheddar cheese, grated
1 spring onion, finely chopped
1 tbsp chopped fresh parsley
70g wholemeal flour
3 eggs, lightly beaten
120ml full fat milk

Tip: To prepare this recipe as a pancake simply follow my instructions on page 176.

1. Preheat your waffle maker.

2. Add the grated carrot, sweet potato, cheese, spring onion, parsley and wholemeal flour into a large mixing bowl and stir until combined.

3. Add the eggs and milk and mix well.

4. Pour a ladle of the mixture in the centre of the waffle maker and spread a little to the sides. Cook for 3 to 5 minutes or until golden brown.

5. Serve with your favourite toppings.

Spicy Pumpkin Waffles

These waffles are moist, delicious and fluffy and your child will love the spices. They are perfect when the weather is cold, but can be enjoyed any time of the year. You can swap the pumpkin for any type of squash.

Makes: 6 Waffles

65g wholemeal flour
95g self raising flour
1 tsp cinnamon
1 tsp ground ginger
240ml full fat milk
1 tbsp olive oil
1 egg
60g pumpkin, baked and puréed

Tip: Pumpkin can be baked with the skin on to save you peeling. Just make sure to remove it before puréeing!

1. Preheat your waffle iron.

2. Mix all the dry ingredients in a bowl and make a well.

3. In another bowl, whisk the milk, oil and egg together. Add the wet ingredients to the dry and mix well.

4. Add the puréed pumpkin and stir.

5. Pour a ladle of the mixture in the centre of the waffle maker and spread a little to the sides. Cook for 3 to 5 minutes or until golden brown.

6. Serve with your favourite toppings.

Snacks

Healthy snacks are essential in your child's lunchbox. We don't always have time to prepare homemade snacks so make sure when choosing shop bought that they are low in salt and sugar and free from preservatives. Homemade popcorn is the perfect snack for a school lunch and you can easily prepare it before school.

Popcorn 3 Ways

This is such an easy snack to prepare and the girls are always excited to see it in their lunchbox. I have listed three options but there are so many ways to change this up by using ingredients like turmeric, caramel or chocolate. Popcorn is the perfect snack and homemade isn't bad for you. In fact popcorn kernels are actually wholegrain and are rich in fibre.

Makes: 4 Adult Portions

3 tbsp vegetable oil
2 tbsp popcorn kernels
½ tsp salt

Salted Popcorn
As the recipe states

Buttered Popcorn
1-2 tbsp butter

Parmesan Popcorn
50g Parmesan

1. Heat the vegetable oil in a large saucepan over a medium heat. Add the popcorn kernels making sure they are evenly distributed on the base of the pan and immediately place the lid on the pan.

2. Gently shake the pan every 10 seconds (the popcorn kernels should start popping). As soon as they stop popping remove from the heat.

3. Pour the popcorn into a large bowl. Add in your salt

For Buttered Popcorn:
Add the butter at step 1 after you add the popcorn kernels.

For Parmesan Popcorn
After you remove the popcorn add in your salt and your Parmesan cheese. Toss to combine.

Yoghurt Fruit Dips 3 Ways

I started making this for my girls when they were small so that they could learn how to eat finger foods with a dip (yoghurt) and a dipper (a piece of fruit). These are a great alternative to offering flavoured yoghurts which can be high in sugar.

Makes: 1 Fruit Dip Portion

Orange Greek Yoghurt Fruit Dip
125g Greek yoghurt
1½ tbsp honey
1 orange zested
¼ tsp vanilla extract

Chocolate Greek Yoghurt Fruit Dip
125g Greek yoghurt
1½ tbsp honey
1 tbsp cocoa powder
¼ tsp vanilla extract
A pinch of cinnamon

Nut Butter Greek Yoghurt Fruit Dip
125g Greek yoghurt
1½ tbsp honey
1 tbsp nut butter (pg 173)
¼ tsp vanilla extract
A pinch of cinnamon

Serve with:
Apple slices, bananas, pears
Plain rice cakes

1. For each flavour mix your ingredients together by whipping them together with a spoon.

2. Keep in your portion pots and serve with your child's favourite fruit and/or rice cakes.

Cheese Biscuits

I have been making these biscuits since the girls were toddlers. They are low in salt and contain no sugar - not sure if they are therefore allowed to be called a biscuit! I usually cut them into heart shapes which adds that extra little touch when packing a lunchbox.

Makes: 12-16 Biscuits

30g butter
130g self raising flour, plus extra for dusting
120g Cheddar cheese, grated
30ml full fat milk
1 egg

1. Preheat your oven to 180°C.

2. With your fingers, rub the butter into the flour until the mixture resembles breadcrumbs. Stir in the grated cheese. Then add in the milk and egg until the mixture forms a dough.

3. Dust a clean surface, your hands and the dough with a little flour. Gently flatten the dough with a rolling pin until it is approx 3cm thick. Use a cutter or a knife to cut out biscuits of your desired shape. Re-roll and re-cut any extra dough.

4. Grease a baking tray and transfer the biscuits onto it. Bake for 12-15 minutes, until they are golden brown and well risen.

5. Once cooled, store fresh in an airtight container for a week or freeze for future use.

Vegetable Crisps

Wonderfully colourful, you will love these tasty vegetable crisps.

Makes: 8 Portions

500g sweet potato
350g parsnip
400g beetroot
Rosemary, finely chopped
Salt
Olive oil

1. Preheat the oven to 200°C. Line a baking tray with parchment paper.

2. Wash, peel and cut each vegetable in half. Using a knife, mandolin or a vegetable peeler slice the vegetables as thin as possible. The thinner they are, the crispier they will become.

3. Place all the sliced vegetables in a bowl with the herbs and salt. Drizzle with olive oil and mix well until both sides are well coated.

4. Arrange the vegetable slices on a baking tray. Bake for 20 minutes, turning occasionally. You want the slices to be dry and crispy, but not burnt!

5. Allow to cool before serving.

Roasted Savoury Chickpeas

This is such a versatile snack and I have been making combinations of this recipe since my children were babies. There are lots of interesting flavours here that your child is sure to love.

Makes: 4 Portions

400g tin chickpeas
½ tsp ground cumin
½ tsp smoked paprika
½ tsp garlic powder
Pinch onion powder
Pinch ground coriander
½ tsp salt
¼ tsp ground black pepper
1 tsp olive oil

1. Preheat oven to 200°C and line a baking tray with parchment paper.

2. Drain, rinse and pat the chickpeas dry.

3. Place them on the tray and roast in the oven for 40 minutes, or until dried out.

4. Meanwhile, combine all the spices and seasonings in a bowl.

5. Remove the chickpeas from the oven. Toss in your mix and drizzle with the oil.

6. Roast for a further 5-10 minutes until they become crispy.

7. Eat immediately, or store in an airtight portion pot for up to one week.

Roasted Sweet Chickpeas

This recipe is high in protein and fibre and it's also a healthy sweet snack! My girls are extra pleased when they see this in their lunchbox. Make plenty and store in your airtight portion pots for up to a week.

Makes: 4 Portions

400g tin chickpeas
½ tsp cinnamon
Pinch of nutmeg
Pinch of salt
1 tbsp honey
½ tbsp olive oil

1. Preheat oven to 200°C and line a baking tray with parchment paper.

2. Drain, rinse and pat the chickpeas dry.

3. Place the chickpeas on the tray and roast for 40 minutes, or until dried out.

4. Meanwhile, in a bowl combine the spices, salt, honey and olive oil.

5. Remove the chickpeas from the oven and toss in your mix.

6. Roast for a further 5-10 minutes until they become crispy.

Healthy Granola Bars

Granola bars are so easy and perfect as an afternoon snack. If you wrap and store them individually they are just as convenient as shop bought alternatives and even more nutritious.

Makes: 12 Bars

4 tbsp butter or coconut oil
6 tbsp fruit purée, I used apple
2 tbsp honey or maple syrup
180g porridge oats
4 tbsp mixed seeds
3 tbsp ground almonds
2 tbsp pecans, finely chopped

Optional extra:
Handful of raisins
Chocolate chips

1. Preheat your oven to 180°C. Line a baking tray with parchment paper.

2. Melt the coconut oil or butter in a small saucepan over a low heat. Stir in the fruit purée and honey or maple syrup then heat gently.

3. Combine all of the dry ingredients in a large bowl.

4. Add in the wet ingredients and stir to combine.

5. Spread the granola mixture on the lined tray and shape it into a rectangle about 2 cm thick.

6. Bake in the oven for 15-20 minutes until golden brown.

7. Remove from the oven and allow to fully cool before cutting into squares.

8. Wrap individually in parchment paper and store in airtight portion pots for up to a week.

Make Your Own Trail Mix

You will most likely have all the ingredients for a trail mix in your cupboard so it's all about putting it together. Let your child make it up so that they are keen on eating it. Have one for home with nuts and one for school without nuts using two portions of seeds instead.

Makes: 1 Portion

1 tbsp of nuts of choice:
Almonds, pistachios, cashews, peanuts, walnuts, hazelnuts, brazil nuts, pecans or pine nuts

1 tbsp of seeds of choice:
Pumpkin seeds, sunflower seeds, flaxseed or sesame seeds

1 tbsp of cereal of choice:
Granola (pg 49), popcorn (pg 187), crackers (smashed), cheerios or sesame sticks

1 tbsp of dried fruit of choice:
Dried Cranberries, raisins, pineapple, banana or apricots

1 tbsp of your choice of extras:
(optional)
Shredded coconut, chocolate chips, sprinkle of sea salt, cinnamon or nutmeg

1. Mix your nuts, seeds, cereal, dried fruit and extras if using, together. Portion into an airtight container, ready for your child's snack time.

Almond Butter Balls

I love to have these on hand when we are running between school and our after school activities. They provide the perfect energy boost for your child.

Makes: 15 Balls

150g almond butter (pg 173)
90g honey
90g porridge oats
2 tbsp ground flaxseed

Tip: Stick a carrot stick into the base to make them into a lollipop!

1. Place all the ingredients into a food processor and blend until combined.

2. Remove the mixture and shape into bite sized balls.

3. Store in airtight portion pots for up to one week or freeze for future use.

SNACKS

Pickled Vegetables

I have to credit my good friend Aideen for introducing my family to homemade pickled vegetables. When she came to stay with us she brought a lovely jar of home-made pickled cucumber. My girls like the taste of vinegar and are keen on most vegetables so I thought it might be good to give my own recipe a try. My advice is to get your child involved in the prep work using their favourite vegetable and you will be surprised how much they like it. My 480ml/16oz Mummy Cooks portion pots work best for this recipe.

Makes: 2 x 480ml Portions

450g Vegetables
Cucumber, thinly sliced
Yellow squash, thinly sliced
Carrots, cut into spears
Green beans or asparagus
Cherry tomatoes

For the Brine
4 cloves of garlic, sliced
2 sprigs fresh herbs, such as thyme, dill, or rosemary
2 tsp mustard seeds or peppercorns
250ml white wine or cider vinegar
250ml water
1 tbsp sugar
1 tbsp salt

1. Prepare your vegetables; wash, peel and cut into the desired shape.

2. Divide your garlic, herbs and mustard seeds or peppercorns into two 480ml pots.

3. Then divide the vegetables into each pot whether you are using a mixture or just one. Pack them in as tightly as you can without smashing.

4. Combine the vinegar, water, salt, and sugar in a small saucepan over a high heat. Bring to the boil, stirring to dissolve. Pour the brine over the vegetables, filling each pot to within 1cm of the top. You might not use all the brine.

5. Let the pots cool to room temperature then refrigerate. The pickles will improve with flavour as they age, wait at least 48 hours before opening. Use in sandwiches or simply as a snack in your child's lunchbox.

Smoothies

Smoothies are an ideal snack or accompaniment to a meal for growing children. There are some children who don't like the crunch of an apple and would much prefer to drink a smoothie. Serve cold in your child's chilled food flask and it will be perfect for a mid-morning snack. I have included a variety of smoothies from carrot and orange to a nutty mango surprise.

The Hulk Smoothie

This Spinach, Apple and Ginger Smoothie is a really great way of getting your child's five a day early in the morning to set them up for the day ahead. Think about adding this to your child's food flask for an extra nutritious snack.

Makes: 1 Adult Portion

½ apple peeled, cored and chopped
5 slices of cucumber
Juice of half a lemon
1 tbsp ginger, grated
1 large handful spinach
1 tbsp chia seeds
Handful of ice cubes

Tip: Serve over ice for a refreshing cold drink.

1. Place all of the ingredients in a smoothie maker or blender and blend until smooth. Add more water if needed.

Purple Madness

This smoothie provides a totally balanced breakfast or snack. Your child will love the vibrant purple colour. In the summer months you can freeze this in ice lolly moulds for a cool and refreshing healthy treat.

Makes: 1 Adult Portion

1 orange, juiced
½ pear, peeled, cored and chopped
80g blackberries, fresh or frozen
30g porridge oats
200ml almond milk
1 tbsp of sunflower seeds
Handful of ice cubes

1. Place all of the ingredients in a smoothie maker or blender and blend until smooth. Add more water if needed.

Peaches & Cream Smoothie

A twist on a summer classic - this is a great way to boost your child's vitamin C levels. When peaches are in season they are so delicious, if you have a reluctant fruit eater get them to give this a try and they will be begging for more.

Makes: 2 Adult Portions

250g peaches, fresh or frozen
235ml almond milk or milk of choice
2 tbsp orange juice
Small handful of ice

1. Place all of the ingredients in a smoothie maker or blender and blend until smooth. Add the ice at the end and add more milk if needed.

Tip: To keep your smoothie nice and cold for a school snack place in your child's chilled food flask.

Carrot & Orange Smoothie

Add a boost of vitamin C to your child's day with this refreshing Carrot and Orange Smoothie. A great way to get your child's daily dose of fruits and vegetables.

Makes: 2 Adult Portions

230ml orange juice
120g Greek yoghurt
45g porridge oats
1 carrot, peeled and sliced
170g pineapple, chopped

Tip: Double up and store in an airtight container in the fridge. Make sure to fill it to the top so that there is no air as air oxidizes the nutrients.

1. Place all of the ingredients in a smoothie maker or blender and blend until smooth. Add more orange juice or water if needed.

Nutty Mango Surprise

A really easy, delicious smoothie that tastes more like a shake. This smoothie is just the thing to convert reluctant smoothie drinkers.

Makes: 2 Adult Portions

240ml orange juice
125g natural yoghurt
2 mangoes, chopped
1 banana
30g porridge oats
1 tbsp nut butter (pg 173)

1. Place all of the ingredients in a smoothie maker or blender and blend until smooth. Add more orange juice or water if needed.

Chocolate Chip Smoothie

This recipe does sound like it should be in the treat section but it's actually really nutritious. Swap out the nut butter for a seed butter and you can pop it in your child's flask as a cool Friday treat.

Makes: 2 Adult Portions

460g natural yoghurt
65g nut butter (pg 173)
355ml full fat milk
45g chocolate chips
½ tsp vanilla extract
2 tbsp cocoa powder
Handful of ice

1. Place all of the ingredients in a smoothie maker or blender and blend until smooth. Add the ice at the end and add more milk if needed.

Treats

In this section I have included some recipes for the occasional treat be it 'Treat Friday' at school or a weekend treat. My girls love to bake and so most of the recipes in this section are recipes that we have come up with together. Enjoy!

Oaty Chocolate Chip Cookies

These cookies are extra crunchy with the addition of porridge oats. My girls love making these cookies for the school cake sale and they always get snapped up.

Makes: 16 Cookies

125g butter, softened
100g light brown sugar
1 egg
1 tsp vanilla extract
150g self raising flour
75g porridge oats
100g milk chocolate chips

Tip: Add some toasted slivers of almonds, which tastes delicious in fresh cookies.

1. Preheat the oven to 190°C and line a baking tray with parchment paper.

2. Put the butter, sugar, egg and vanilla extract into a bowl and beat well.

3. Add in the flour, oats and chocolate chips and mix well.

4. Place spoonfuls of the mixture on your baking tray leaving a space as they will spread while cooking.

5. Bake for 15 minutes or until they begin to turn brown.

6. Allow them to cool slightly, then carefully turn out onto a wire rack to cool completely.

7. Serve straight away or keep for up to 5 days in an airtight container.

Peanut Butter Cookies

With just three ingredients these cookies are the perfect quick snack that your children will love. Drizzle some melted chocolate on top for extra deliciousness.

Makes: 16 Cookies

280g peanut butter (pg 173)
1 egg
2 tbsp honey or maple syrup

Tip: If you want to add some texture to your cookies, use crunchy peanut butter.

1. Preheat the oven to 180°C and line a baking tray with parchment paper.

2. In a bowl, add the peanut butter, egg and honey or syrup. Mix well, until it firms up to a cookie dough consistency.

3. Using a teaspoon, take spoonfuls of the dough and roll into a ball with your hands. Place on the baking tray and gently press down to form a disc shape.

4. Bake in the oven for 8-15 minutes.

5. Let the cookies cool completely before serving. Store in an airtight container for up to 5 days.

Gingerbread Cookies

These make a really lovely homemade gift at Christmas. My girls love to bake Gingerbread Cookies every year and wrap them up in pretty paper and ribbon to give to their teachers. They especially love decorating them!

Makes: 15 Cookies

75g butter, softened
75g brown sugar
1 egg
2 tbsp maple syrup
250g plain flour
½ tsp baking powder
1 tsp cinnamon
1 tsp ground ginger

Decorations:
Melted chocolate
Icing pens
Cake decorations

1. Preheat the oven to 180°C and line a baking tray with parchment paper.

2. Cream the butter and sugar together until light and fluffy.

3. Add in the egg and maple syrup and mix through.

4. Sift the flour, baking powder and spices in a separate bowl.

5. Combine the wet and dry ingredients into a dough and place in the fridge for a minimum of 30 minutes.

6. Roll the dough out into a thin layer and cut into desired shapes.

7. Place on your baking tray and bake in the oven for 15-20 minutes until golden.

8. Allow to cool completely on a wire rack before decorating.

Courgette Brownies

Adding courgette may sound a bit strange, but it makes these chocolate treats super moist, and you won't even know it's in there! You may win the favourite parent award with these.

Makes: 12 Brownies

200g butter
300g caster sugar
100g cocoa
3 eggs, lightly beaten
100g self raising flour
350g courgette, grated

1. Preheat the oven to 180°C. Grease a 20cm square cake tin and set aside.

2. In a large saucepan over a low heat, melt the butter then add the sugar and cocoa. Leave to cool.

3. Add in the eggs little by little, then add the flour and courgette and mix to combine.

4. Pour the mixture into your cake tin and bake on the top shelf of your oven for 35 minutes until a knife inserted comes out clean.

5. Transfer to a wire rack and allow to cool before slicing into brownies.

Mini Mug Cakes

Not only are these child-friendly mug cakes refined-sugar free, they are so easy and quick to make. You can even cook them in the microwave!

Makes: 1 Mini Mug Cake

4 tbsp self raising flour
1 egg
3 tbsp full fat milk
3 tbsp vegetable oil
½ tsp vanilla extract
1 tbsp maple syrup

Double chocolate
2 tbsp cocoa
1 tbsp chocolate chips

Blueberry vanilla
Handful of fresh blueberries

Tip: While I used oven safe ramekins if using a mug make sure its microwave and/or oven safe.

1. If baking in the oven, preheat the oven to 180°C.

2. In a large mug or mini ramekin dish, place all the dry ingredients and mix well with a spoon. Use the spoon to grind all of the cocoa (if using) and flour against the side of the mug so there are no lumps.

3. Add the egg and beat it a little on top of the dry ingredients to break the yolk.

4. Add the oil, milk, vanilla and maple syrup. Mix until well combined.

5. Stir in the chocolate chips or blueberries. Put the mug or ramekin into the microwave on high for 3 minutes or place in the oven for 15-25 minutes. Leave to cool slightly before serving.

Bake Sale Cupcakes

Cupcakes are great to make for the school cake sale or any celebration and you can adjust the colour of the buttercream icing and cake decorations to suit the occasion. Your children will love getting involved in making these and if they are anything like mine they will be licking the bowl clean!

Makes: 12 Cupcakes

110g butter, softened
150g caster sugar
2 eggs
1½ tsp vanilla extract
190g plain flour
1 ½ tsp baking powder
½ tsp salt
115g Greek yoghurt

To decorate:
125g butter, softened
225g icing sugar
A few drops vanilla extract
Cake decorations

1. Preheat the oven to 180°C. Grease a muffin or cupcake tin or line with paper cases.

2. Beat the butter and sugar together until light and fluffy. Gradually beat in the eggs and the vanilla extract.

3. Gently fold in the flour, baking powder, salt and yoghurt with a spoon and combine well.

4. Place spoonfuls of the mixture into the cupcake tin and bake for 20 minutes until a knife inserted into the centre comes out clean.

5. Remove from the oven and leave to cool on a wire tray.

6. Make buttercream by beating the butter, icing sugar and vanilla extract together until smooth and creamy.

7. Pipe or swirl icing onto each cupcake then top with cake decorations.

Berry & Almond Bake

In the summer, I love finding creative ways to use the wide variety of fresh seasonal fruits like strawberries, blackberries and blueberries. This quick and easy Berry and Almond Bake is perfect to make from May to August, but can also be enjoyed using frozen berries during the other months. You'll be amazed at how easy it is to make a nutritious and delicious dessert that your whole family will love! It's healthy enough to add to your child's lunchbox.

Makes: 6 Adult Portions

360ml full fat milk
2 eggs
1 tbsp vanilla extract
1 tbsp butter, softened
3 apples, steamed and puréed
180g porridge oats
1 tsp cinnamon
1 tsp baking powder
½ tsp salt
400g mixed berries, fresh or frozen
40g almonds, chopped

1. Preheat the oven to 190°C.

2. In a bowl, whisk the milk, eggs, vanilla extract and butter until combined. Stir in the apple purée.

3. In a separate bowl, combine the oats, cinnamon, baking powder, and salt.

4. Spread half the berries over the bottom of a baking dish. Add the dry mixture evenly over the berries, then pour in the wet mixture. Top with the remaining berries and chopped almonds.

5. Bake in the preheated oven for 40-45 minutes, or until a knife inserted into the centre comes out clean.

Fruit Roll-Ups

A great way of adding fruit to your child's lunchbox, these fruit roll-ups can be made with a variety of different fruits. Your child will love making these with you. We have tried this with pineapple, strawberries and raspberries, and they have all worked a treat!

Makes: 7 Strips

700g strawberries, pineapple or raspberries (on its own or mixed)
1 tbsp of honey

Tip: Treat Fruit Roll-Ups like a sweet treat. Their sticky consistency will cling to teeth so make sure your child brushes soon afterwards.

1. Preheat your oven to 80°C and line a baking tray with parchment paper or use a silicone baking mat.

2. Place your chosen fruit and honey in a blender and purée until smooth.

3. Pour the mixture onto the baking tray and use the back of a spatula to spread it very evenly into a rectangular shape.

4. Bake in the oven for 3 to 4 hours, or until the fruit is dry and not sticky to touch.

5. Cool at room temperature, this may take a few hours to soften up. I usually leave it overnight. Then using a scissors cut into strips keeping it in the paper. Roll it up and pop it into your child's lunchbox.

Ashleigh's Lemonade

When lemons are plentiful and the weather is nice there is nothing better than a glass of lemonade. Ashleigh especially loves this and is always keen to make it when we have visitors over.

Makes: 8 Glasses

10 lemons juiced
1 litre water
400g caster sugar
Handful of ice

Tip: Let the lemonade cool down and refrigerate before serving for an even colder refreshing drink.

1. Juice the fresh lemons to make up 500ml of lemon juice.

2. Make a syrup by adding your water and sugar to a saucepan and cooking over a medium heat until the sugar has dissolved.

3. Combine the syrup with the lemon juice. Add more water to suit your personal taste. Serve over ice.

It doesn't end here

I really hope you've enjoyed my book - my support doesn't end here. Head to **MummyCooks.com** for the latest advice and recipes on feeding your family. Join us on Instagram and Facebook for advice and tips on feeding your child. If you have a weaning baby or are interested in learning more about cooking for the family, check out my book 'Baby & Family; Cook for Family, Adapt for Baby.'

Join our Mummy Cooks Club!
Members get access to guides on feeding your child as well as great recipes, discounts on products and more.
Join for FREE today.

Index

After School Snacking 34

Alfredo Sauce 153

Almond
Almond Butter Balls 200
Berry & Almond Bake 226

Apple
Apple & Banana Muffins 92
Apple & Blueberry Oat Muffins 90
Apple Cinnamon Waffles 181
The Hulk Smoothie 205

Avocado
Avocado Hummus 166
Chicken & Avocado Focaccia 131

Banana
Apple & Banana Muffins 92
Banana Bread 101
Banana & Chocolate Breakfast Cookies 61
Banana French Toast 55
Nut Butter & Chia Seed Toast 56
Oaty Banana Pancakes 178

Batch Cooking 14

Basil
Cucumber, Tomato & Basil Pasta Salad 108
Basil & Courgette Pesto 158
Nut-Free Basil Pesto 159

Beef
One Pot Lasagne 140
Quick Bolognese 137

Berry
Berry & Almond Bake 226

Bircher Muesli 52

Blackberries
Purple Madness 206

Blueberries
Apple & Blueberry Oat Muffins 90
Blueberry Bread 102
Mini Mug Cakes 223

Bolognese
Quick Bolognese 137

Bread
Banana Bread 101
Blueberry Bread 102
Dough Balls 94
Focaccia 98
Lemon Bread 103
Soda Bread 97

Breakfast 47-63

Broccoli
Broccoli Pesto 160
Chicken & Broccoli Bake 138

Brownies
Courgette Brownies 220

Butternut Squash
Curried Butternut Squash Soup 81
Slow Cooker Butternut Squash Lasagne 139

Cabbage
Coleslaw 110

Cakes
Bake Sale Cupcakes 224
Mini Mug Cakes 223

Carbohydrates 18

Index

Carbonara
    Easy Carbonara 151

Carrot
    Carrot & Lentil Soup with Croutons 72
    Carrot & Orange Smoothie 208
    Hearty Vegetable Soup 71
    Potato & Carrot Waffles 182
    Spicy Bean & Carrot Spread 168
    Sweet Potato & Carrot Soup 67

Cauliflower
    Curried Cauliflower & Cheese Soup 80
    Cauliflower Macaroni & Cheese 147

Cereal
    Messy Jessie Cereal Bars 62

Cheese
    Cauliflower Macaroni & Cheese 147
    Cheese Biscuits 189
    Cheese Scones 85
    Chicken Quesadillas 123
    Curried Cauliflower & Cheese Soup 80
    Easy Carbonara 151
    Ham & Cheese Muffins 93
    Mozzarella Pesto Melt 125
    Pesto & Feta Puff Wheels 86
    Salmon & Cream Cheese Pinwheels 120
    Tomato & Mascarpone Sauce 150
    Vegetable Egg Muffins 89
    Veggie Tortilla Roll-Ups 122

Chia Seeds
    Nut Butter and Chia Seed Toast 56
    Overnight Berry & Chia Seed Oats 50

Chicken
    Chicken & Avocado Focaccia 131
    Chicken & Broccoli Bake 138
    Chicken Noodle Soup 75
    Chicken Quesadillas 123
    Chicken Soup 76

Chickpeas
    Avocado Hummus 166
    Classic Hummus 167
    Roasted Savoury Chickpeas 194
    Roasted Sweet Chickpeas 195
    Smashed Chickpea & Roasted Pepper Sandwich 128
    Smashed Chickpea Spread 169
    Tomato & Chickpea Pasta Salad 109

Chocolate
    Banana & Chocolate Breakfast Cookies 61
    Chocolate Chip Smoothie 212
    Chocolate Spread 170
    Courgette Brownies 220
    Messy Jessie Cereal Bars 62
    Mini Mug Cakes 223
    Oaty Chocolate Chip Cookies 216

Cinnamon
    Apple Cinnamon Waffles 181
    Cinnamon Breakfast Energy Balls 58

Coleslaw 110

Cookies
    Banana & Chocolate Breakfast Cookies 61
    Gingerbread Cookies 219
    Oaty Chocolate Chip Cookies 216
    Peanut Butter Cookies 217

Courgette
    Basil & Courgette Pesto 158
    Courgette Brownies 220

Cream Cheese
    Smoked Salmon & Cream Cheese Pinwheels 120

Croutons
    Carrot & Lentil Soup with Croutons 72

Index

Couscous
Fruity Couscous 114

Cucumber
Cucumber, Tomato & Basil Pasta Salad 108
Mediterranean Pita Pocket 132
The Hulk Smoothie 205

Dough Balls 94

Eggs
Banana French Toast 55
Easy Carbonara 151
Omelette Wrap 127
Vegetable Egg Muffins 89
Vegetable Omelette 53

Energy Balls 58

Feta
Pesto & Feta Puff Wheels 86

Focaccia
Focaccia Bread 98
Chicken & Avocado Focaccia 131

Food Labels 38
Food Preparation 14
Food Safety 40

Freezer
Stocking 40

French Toast
Banana French Toast 55

Fruit 19, 22-23
Fruity Couscous 114
Fruit Roll-Ups 227
Fruit Wraps 57

Gazpacho 77

Gingerbread Cookies 219

Granola
Healthy Granola Bars 197
Nut-Free Granola 49

Ham
Ham & Cheese Muffins 93

Herbs & Spices 41

Hummus
Avocado Hummus 166
Classic Hummus 167

Kebabs
Sandwich Kebabs 119

Labels 38

Lasagne
One Pot Lasagne 140
Slow Cooker Butternut Squash Lasagne 139

Lemon
Ashleigh's Lemonade 228
Lemon Bread 103

Lentils
Carrot & Lentil Soup 72

Macaroni
Cauliflower Macaroni & Cheese 147

Mango
Nutty Mango Surprise 211

Marinara Sauce 148

Mascarpone
Tomato & Mascarpone Sauce 150

Index

Mint
    Pea & Mint Soup 68

Mozzarella
    Mozzarella Pesto Melt 125

Muesli
    Bircher Muesli 52

Muffins
    Apple & Banana Muffins 92
    Apple & Blueberry Oat Muffins 90
    Ham & Cheese Muffins 93
    Vegetable Egg Muffins 89

Noodles
    Chicken Noodle Soup 75

Nut Butter
    Almond Butter Balls 200
    Banana & Chocolate Breakfast Cookies 61
    Cinnamon Breakfast Energy Balls 58
    Nut Butter 173
    Nut Butter & Chia Seed Toast 56
    Peanut Butter Cookies 217

Oats
    Almond Butter Balls 200
    Apple & Blueberry Oat Muffins 90
    Banana & Chocolate Breakfast Cookies 61
    Bircher Muesli 52
    Carrot & Orange Smoothie 208
    Cinnamon Breakfast Energy Balls 58
    Nut-Free Granola 49
    Healthy Granola Bars 197
    Oaty Banana Pancakes 178
    Oaty Chocolate Chip Cookies 216
    Overnight Berry & Chia Seed Oats 50
    Purple Madness 206

Olives
    Mediterranean Pita Pocket 132

Pancakes
    Pancake Sandwiches 176
    Oaty Banana Pancakes 178
    Sweetcorn Pancakes 177

Parsnip
    Curried Parsnip & Pear Soup 78

Pasta
    Alfredo Sauce 153
    Cauliflower Macaroni & Cheese 147
    Chicken & Broccoli Bake 138
    Cucumber, Tomato & Basil Pasta Salad 108
    Easy Carbonara 151
    Easy Peasy Tortelloni 144
    Marinara Sauce 148
    Quick Bolognese 137
    Roasted Red Pepper & Sweetcorn Pasta Salad 107
    Roasted Vegetable Pasta Bake 143
    Tomato & Chickpea Pasta Salad 109
    Tomato & Mascarpone Sauce 150

Pea
    Easy Peasy Tortelloni 144
    Pea & Mint Soup 68

Peach
    Peaches & Cream Smoothie 207

Peanut
    Peanut Butter Cookies 217

Pear
    Curried Parsnip & Pear Soup 78

Pepper
    Red Pepper Pesto 161
    Roasted Red Pepper & Sweetcorn Pasta Salad 107
    Smashed Chickpea & Roasted Pepper Sandwich 128

Index

Pesto
    Basil & Courgette Pesto 158
    Broccoli Pesto 160
    Mozzarella Pesto Melt 125
    Nut-Free Basil Pesto 159
    Pesto & Feta Puff Wheels 86
    Red Pepper Pesto 161

Pickled Vegetables 201

Picky Eater 36

Pita Bread
    Mediterranean Pita Pocket 132

Popcorn 3 Ways 187

Potato
    Potato & Carrot Waffles 182
    Potato Salad 113

Portion Pots 16

Protein 18, 24-25

Pumpkin
    Spicy Pumpkin Waffles 183

Quesadillas
    Chicken Quesadillas 123

Salad
    Coleslaw 110
    Cucumber, Tomato & Basil Pasta Salad 108
    Potato Salad 113
    Roasted Red Pepper & Sweetcorn Pasta Salad 107
    Tomato & Chickpea Pasta Salad 109

Salsa
    Tomato Salsa & Crispy Tortilla 163

Salmon
    Smoked Salmon & Cream Cheese Pinwheels 120

Sandwiches
    Chicken & Avocado Focaccia 131
    Mediterranean Pita Pocket 132
    Mozzarella Pesto Melt 125
    Sandwich Kebabs 119
    Smashed Chickpea & Roasted Pepper Sandwich 128
    Tuna & Sweetcorn Sandwich 126

Sauces
    Alfredo Sauce 153
    Basil & Courgette Pesto 158
    Broccoli Pesto 160
    Easy Carbonara 151
    Marinara Sauce 148
    Nut-Free Basil Pesto 159
    Quick Bolognese 137
    Red Pepper Pesto 161
    Tomato & Mascarpone Sauce 150

Schedule 42

Scones
    Cheese Scones 85

Senses 28

Slow Cooker
    Slow Cooker Butternut Squash Lasagne 139

Smoothies
    Carrot Orange Smoothie 208
    Chocolate Chip Smoothie 212
    Nutty Mango Surprise 211
    Peaches & Cream Smoothie 207
    Purple Madness 206
    The Hulk Smoothie 205

Index

Snacking 34, 185

Soup 65-81
    Carrot & Lentil Soup 72
    Chicken Noodle Soup 75
    Chicken Soup 76
    Curried Butternut Squash Soup 81
    Curried Cauliflower & Cheese Soup 80
    Curried Parsnip & Pear Soup 78
    Gazpacho 77
    Hearty Vegetable Soup 71
    Pea & Mint Soup 68
    Sweet Potato & Carrot Soup 67

Spreads
    Chocolate Spread 170
    Spicy Bean & Carrot Spread 168
    Smashed Chickpea Spread 169

Sweetcorn
    Roasted Red Pepper & Sweetcorn Pasta
    Salad 107
    Sweetcorn Pancakes 177
    Tuna & Sweetcorn Sandwich 126

Sweet Potato
    Sweet Potato & Carrot Soup 67

Toast
    Banana French Toast 55
    Nut Butter & Chia Seed Toast 56

Tomato
    Cucumber, Tomato & Basil Pasta Salad 108
    Gazpacho 77
    Marinara Sauce 148
    Spicy Tomato Sauce 155
    Tomato & Chickpea Pasta Salad 109
    Tomato & Mascarpone Sauce 150
    Tomato Salsa & Crispy Tortilla 163
    Tomato Sauce 154

Tortelloni
    Easy Peasy Tortelloni 144

Tortilla
    Tomato Salsa & Crispy Tortilla 163
    Veggie Tortilla Roll-ups 122

Trail Mix
    Make your own Trail Mix 198

Tuna
    Tuna & Sweetcorn Sandwich 126

Vegetables 19, 20-21
    Vegetable Crisps 190
    Vegetable Egg Muffins 89
    Vegetable Omelette 53
    Roasted Vegetables Pasta Bake 143
    Pickled Vegetables 201
    Veggie Tortilla Roll-Ups 122
    Hearty Vegetable Soup 71

Waffles
    Apple Cinnamon Waffles 181
    Potato & Carrot Waffles 182
    Spicy Pumpkin Waffles 183

Wraps
    Chicken Quesadillas 123
    Fruit wraps 57
    Omelette Wrap 127
    Veggie Tortilla Roll-ups 122

Yoghurt
    Apple & Blueberry Oat Muffins 90
    Bircher Muesli 52
    Carrot & Orange Smoothie 208
    Chocolate Chip Smoothie 212
    Fruit wraps 57
    Nutty Mango Surprise 211
    Yoghurt Fruit Dips 3 Ways 188

About Siobhan Berry

Siobhan Berry is the founder and creator of the popular website MummyCooks.com, where she helps parents every day to feed their children nutritious home-cooked foods. Siobhan is SOS trained for strategies on feeding fussy or problem eaters and the author of 'Baby and Family; Cook for Family, Adapt for Baby' recipe book.

As a working mum, bringing up a family, she understands the issues families and busy households face when it comes to packing healthy lunchboxes day after day. Her food philosophy is simple: she believes that preparation through batch cooking is the key to creating healthy home-cooked meals for the family. This includes lunchbox meals for children.

Siobhan makes regular appearances on Ireland AM breakfast television promoting tasty and healthy dishes for families.

Siobhan lives in Dublin, Ireland with her husband and two children.